SAFETY-CRITICAL REAL-TIME SYSTEMS

edited by

Bernd Krämer
Norbert Völker
FernUniversität
Hagen, Germany

A Special Issue of
REAL-TIME SYSTEMS
The International Journal of
Time-Critical Computing Systems
Volume 13, No. 3 (1997)

KLUWER ACADEMIC PUBLISHERS
Boston / Dordrecht / London

REAL-TIME SYSTEMS

The International
Journal of
Time-Critical
Computing Systems

Volume 13, No. 3, November 1997

Special Issue on Safety-Critical Systems
Guest Editors: Bernd Krämer and Norbert Völker

Distributors for North America:
Kluwer Academic Publishers
101 Philip Drive
Assinippi Park
Norwell, Massachusetts 02061 USA

Distributors for all other countries:
Kluwer Academic Publishers Group
Distribution Centre
Post Office Box 322
3300 AH Dordrecht, THE NETHERLANDS

ISBN 978-1-4419-5019-2

Library of Congress Cataloging-in-Publication Data

A C.I.P. Catalogue record for this book is available
from the Library of Congress.

Printed on acid-free paper.

Real-Time Systems, 13, 217–218 (1997)

Editorial

BERND J. KRÄMER   bernd.kraemer@fernuni-hagen.de
FernUniversität, Faculty of Electrical Engineering, D-58084 Hagen, Germany

Introduction

An increasing number of safety critical systems are controlled by more and more complex software. In these systems program design and coding errors, failures of technical components, or errors of human operators can cause fatal accidents including loss of human life, personal injury, or significant environmental damage. The growing awareness of our society of the need to protect the environment, a higher sensitivity to accidents caused by ill-designed technology or processes, and a declining trust in marketing statements of manufacturers produce an enormous pressure to increase the dependability, reliability, and availability of safety critical applications. Emerging standards and enforced legal requirements in typical application areas such as process automation, medical systems, traffic surveillance and control, or reactor supervision mirror these economic and social changes.

Often safety critical systems are *reactive* and *time critical*, i.e., they must continuously react to external stimuli within predefined time limits. Stimuli may be caused periodically by system clocks or sporadically by remote sensors and client controllers or by operator commands. Safety constraints typically include requirements that the embedded software is responsible for detecting all kinds of hazardous system states and prevent the system to enter unsafe states [1]. Hazardous system states may be raised, for instance, through failures of critical hardware components or the malfunctioning of operating system functions and must be taken into account in the process of software verification. This means that the correctness of the embedded software must be established in the context of both desired and possible behavior of observed and controlled hardware components and in consideration of expected and unexpected human operator interaction.

Survey of the Contributions

The four papers in this special issue provide a selective view on various aspects of safety critical software development and verification.

In the first paper, Mazzeo et al. describe a method to build Petri net models of concurrent systems from trace-based CSP specifications. The strong support for modularization provided by the process algebra CSP opens a more systematic way to build large Petri net specifications. Conversely, this approach allows the authors to benefit from the mature analysis and simulation tools for stochastic timed Petri nets, which are not available to a comparable extent for the timed CSP approach.

The second paper by Krämer and Völker presents a highly dependable computing architecture for safety-critical control applications. This work is based on an international

1

standard for higher level PLC[1] programming languages. The authors exploit the concept of function blocks – which implements the engineer's idea of re-usable "software ICs" – to develop a modular, theorem prover based verification methodology. By taking components from application-specific libraries of verified standard function blocks, the verification of new applications is reduced considerably because only the correctness of the composition has to be established.

Langmaack then surveys the approach to correct systems developed in the ESPRIT project ProCoS – Provably Correct Systems. ProCoS views a technical system as a hybrid entity consisting of control processors, sensors, actuators, connecting channels, and timers which are embedded in a physical environment. The approach is particularly suited for hybrid systems which allow for concurrency and have to satisfy lower and upper time bounds to guarantee maximal and minimal operating rates for hard real-time problems. A major achievement is that formally verified transitions between different levels of system specifications have been defined. In particular, the Duration Calculus has been used to provide a basis for the semantics and verification of both discrete and continuous models.

While the first three papers all deal with formal methods and their applications, the final paper by Wedde and Lind reports on a heuristic, experimental, performance-driven and performance-based methodology for the development of complex safety-critical systems operating in an unpredictable environment. The *Incremental Experimentation* method presented is applied to the design of the distributed operating system MELODY. MELODY exhibits novel services for supporting real-time and safety-critical applications in unpredictable environments.

Notes

1. Programmable Logic Controller.

References

1. Leveson, N.G., "Safeware - System Safety and Computers," Addison-Wesley, 1995.

Real-Time Systems, 13, 219–236 (1997)

A Systematic Approach to the Petri Net Based Specification of Concurrent Systems

ANTONINO MAZZEO   mazzeo@grid.unina.it

NICOLA MAZZOCCA   mazzocca@grid.unina.it

STEFANO RUSSO   russo@grid.unina.it

VALERIA VITTORINI   vittorin@grid.unina.it

Dipartimento di Informatica e Sistemistica, Università di Napoli Via Claudio 21, 80125 Napoli, Italy

Abstract. We describe an approach to the specification of concurrent systems which enables a Petri net model of a system to be built up in a systematic way starting from a trace-based CSP specification. This method enables the separate specification of the behavior of each component (process) and their interactions in terms of the feasible sequences of events in which they can be involved. A set of rules is then applied to transform the trace-based specifications into a complete Petri net that is analyzed and/or executed to validate system behavior. The domain transformation procedure is fully automatable. The specification of a safety-critical railway control system is used as a case study.

Keywords: concurrent software engineering, formal specification and verification, CSP, Petri nets, safety analysis

1. Introduction

In the last decade the development of concurrent software has become a common practice in the high-performance computing community, where it is considered a means of fully exploiting the power of the most advanced computer architectures for compute-intensive problems. However, scientific supercomputing is only one area for concurrent software application, and there has been a strong and increasing demand for concurrent software in the development of real-time control systems, embedded systems, safety-related systems, client-server architectures, and distributed and multimedia systems [6]. However, the production of high-quality, reliable concurrent software in such application areas requires the software engineer to use sound methods. Formal methods can play a crucial role, as they provide the ability to make a qualitative and quantitative analysis of the behavior of a system, in order to assess its correctness and reliability. The clear benefit of a formal model is that it can be mathematically analyzed and solved to prove the properties of the system under development. In most real problems, however, formal model construction is a complex task even for skilled software engineers. Hand-made building of a formal model from an informal description of the system is difficult and error-prone and model construction for concurrent systems is an activity that calls for modular, structured techniques.

Our work addresses the definition of a method to obtain a Petri net based formal specification of a concurrent system in a systematic and rigorous manner. Petri nets (PN) are one of the most mature formalisms used to specify and analyze the behavior of concurrent systems [10]. The proposed method exploits the algebraic basis of the theory of Communicating

3

Sequential Processes (CSP) [5], which allows PNs to be built from a trace-based description of the behavior of the system components and their interactions. Temporal specifications are incorporated at a certain stage of the method to allow system quantitative analysis. The method has the advantage of being able to avoid hand-made PN model construction and enables modular specification and reasoning to be conducted on the various concurrent activities in the system. The PN model is used for system verification, e.g. for deadlock detection or safety analysis, and/or for performance evaluation, depending on the nature of the system under development. The PN can also be executed to simulate the system dynamic behavior. PN analysis and simulation can be carried out using appropriate CASE tools (e.g. [4], [14]).

The goal of this paper is to present the steps and the basic features of the method, and to describe its application by means of a well known case study in the field of safety-critical system design [7]. The method has been developed by the authors in the framework of a joint project with a railway transportation systems company. A complete description of the technical details of the method can be found in [16]. The rest of the paper is organized as follows. In Section 2 we give an overview of the method, concentrating on the rules for the transformation from the trace-based algebraic domain to the PN domain. In Section 3 the method is applied to a classical case study, a railway (train+gate) control system. Finally, in Section 4 we briefly refer to the related work and give some concluding remarks.

2.   Overview of the method

The main feature of the methodology is that a stochastic PN model of a concurrent system is built in a modular and systematic way starting from a trace-based specification. The methodology enables the separate specification of the behavior of each component (process) and their interactions in terms of the feasible sequences of events in which they can be involved.

The steps of the methodology are as follows:

I.   An informal system description is obtained from the requirements (expressed in the natural language). This consists of a list of the components and, for each of these, of a list of events, states and logical or timing constraints. The interactions between components correspond to subsets of common events.

II.   A CSP specification is derived from these lists and expressed as a set of feasible traces, one for each component.

III.   The set of traces is transformed into a set of equivalent PN representations. This is done according to predefined algorithms and rules.

IV.   This step considers the interactions between processes. The Petri subnets modeling the individual processes are integrated, yielding a standard Petri net model of the all system we call PN skeleton. Algorithmic rules are also applied for this purpose.

V.   The PN skeleton is completed by introducing in the model the constraints that involve more components.

4

VI. The PN skeleton is changed into a timed net and supplemented with quantitative parameters. This step is necessary when dealing with real-time systems and whenever time plays an important role in the system analysis.

The reader is assumed to be acquainted with the basic concepts of Petri nets (e.g. see [10]), and the theory of Communicating Sequential Processes [5]. In the remainder of the paper we will use the following notations (see also [5]):

P	process name
S	state name
t	trace name
e	event name
$<>$	empty trace
$< e1 >$	trace containing only the event e1
$< e1, e2 >$	trace containing two events e1 then e2
$\{< e1, e2 >\}^*$	infinite set of traces:
	$\{<>, < e1 >, < e1, e2 >, < e1, e2, e1 >, < e1, e2, e1, e2 >...\}$
$\#t$	length of the trace t
t'	last event in the trace t
t''	trace t deprived of its last event
αP	alphabet of process P
traces(P)	set of all possible traces of the process P
$P\|\|Q$	P in parallel with Q
$P\|\|\|Q$	P interleaved Q

Throughout the paper, processes are denoted by a capital letter, states by a capital letter in italics, events by a lower case letter and traces by a lower case letter in italics. The six steps are described in more detail below.

2.1. Informal system description

In the first step of the method, an informal description is derived from the system requirements, which are often available in the form of documents in the natural language. This informal description must contain all the information needed in the next phase to identify the CSP processes and their feasible traces (in the Hoare sense). Hence, the designer has to specify a list of the system components and for each component:

a) a list of the events in which it can be involved;

b) a list of all its possible states;

c) a list of assumptions on the states;

d) the temporal specifications.

The states are defined through logical predicates in the natural language, which identify the events that cause the transition into a given state. The assumptions represent constraints on the feasible sequences of the events. Internal assumptions are precedence or logical constraints between events of a given process. External assumptions concern events involving

5

more than one process. The temporal specifications consist of a list of the time-consuming events and their related temporal parameters. This list is used to introduce the temporal variable simply and naturally into the system model.

2.2. Definition of the trace-based specifications

In the second step, a formal CSP specification of the system is derived from the informal description. First of all, each component identified by the informal description becomes a process and its set of events becomes its alphabet. The presence of events in more than one alphabet means that their occurrence requires the simultaneous participation of the corresponding processes. A name is assigned to each process, event, state and assumption listed in the informal description. Then the states must be formally defined. Let $L_S(P)$ be the subset of the events of the alphabet αP that cause the transition of the process P into the state S. Every state S is formally defined by a predicate:

$$S(t) \equiv t =<> \lor t' \in \alpha P t \in traces(P)$$

where $S(t)$ denotes all the traces t of the process P whose last event t' belongs to $L_S(P)$. This expression states that P can be in the state S iff the last event occurred in its trace belongs to $L_S(P)$. Finally, the internal and external assumptions must be formally expressed. Let int be the name of an internal assumption on the state S of the process P. int is defined through a boolean expression:

$$int : t' \in L_S(P) \Leftrightarrow S(t")$$

where $S(t")$ denotes all the traces t of P from its initial state to the state before S ($t"$ is t deprived of its last event t'). This definition states that P can be in S iff the trace of P actually belongs to $S(t")$. In other words, int imposes a precedence constraint between two consecutive states of P. We explicitly point out that the internal assumptions, along with the state definitions, make it possible to determine the feasible sequences of events of the process P from its initial state to the final state. The external assumptions express constraints on sequences of events belonging to different processes. Those assumptions which express purely logical constraints (such as precedence or mutual exclusion constraints) could be introduced in the CSP specifications whereas assumptions involving the concept of time cannot be expressed in an untimed logic. In both cases we prefer to introduce external assumptions on the Petri net after the domain transformation, in the fifth step of the method, as this can be achieved using well-known concepts of the PN formalism. Once the states and the assumptions have been formally defined, it is possible to generate the set of legal traces(P) for each process P as a set of event sequences. For example the set:

$$traces(P) = \{<>, < e1 >, < e1, e2 >, < e1, e2, e1 >, < e1, e3 >, < e1, e3, e4 >\}$$

contains six traces, specifying that, after the first event e1, P can evolve in two different ways, involving the sequences e2, e1 or e3, e4.

2.3. Domain transformation

The set of traces of each process is translated into its equivalent PN subnet. This is accomplished by applying translation rules (defined in [16]). This phase can be totally automated by means of a trace-compiler, a tool that translates the trace-based specification of the processes into their equivalent PN representation. For brevity's sake, we present the rules that will be applied in the case study of Section 3. In the following, the transitions are named as the events they represent and the places as the corresponding states. The rules are illustrated graphically in Figure1.

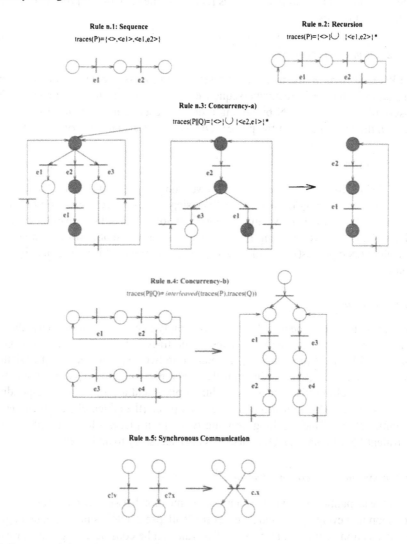

Figure 1. Traces translation rules

- Rule 1: *sequence of events*

  The PN corresponding to a sequence of events merely consists of a sequence of places and transitions. It is obtained from the trace of maximum size, i.e. from $t \in traces(P)$: $max_t(\#t)$. The translation simply consists of associating a transition to each event. The empty trace describes the process before it starts to evolve, and it corresponds to the initial place, whereas the process termination corresponds to a leaf place. According to Hoare [5], a terminating process either terminates successfully, or it becomes impossible for it to be engaged in any of the events of its alphabet. In terms of the PN modeling a sequence of events, a leaf place always represents the state of the process in which no further event occurs.

- Rule 2: *recursive processes*

  The PN equivalent to the trace set of a recursive process is obtained in two steps: a) translation of the basic recursive sequence of events by means of Rule 1; b) cyclic closure of the resulting PN by adding a dummy event corresponding to a transition between the final and the initial places. Of course it is also necessary to add two arcs.

- Rule3: *concurrency-a)*

  The alphabets of the processes P and Q have a not-empty intersection. The equivalent PN of the process P||Q is obtained in three steps: a) separate translation of traces(P) and traces(Q) into their equivalent PN representation; b) identification of the subnet that is common to the two resulting PNs; c) extraction of the subnet which represents the equivalent PN of traces(P||Q). In Figure1 the common subnet is represented by shaded places.

- Rule 4: *concurrency-b)*

  The alphabets of the processes P and Q have empty intersection. In this case the traces of P|||Q are all the possible interleaves of the traces of P and the traces of Q. The equivalent PN of the process P|||Q is obtained in two steps: a) separate translation of traces(P) and traces(Q) into their equivalent PN representation; b) parallel composition of the two resulting PN subnets by adding a place and a transition corresponding to a dummy event. This transition has one input place (the added place which becomes the initial place of the resulting net) and two output places (the initial places of the equivalent PN of P and Q). Of course it is also necessary to add three arcs.

- Rule 5: *synchronous communication*

  Given the semantics of a synchronous communication between two processes, the two corresponding events (send and receive) are "collapsed" into a single one, belonging to the intersection of the two alphabets. This rule can be considered a particular case of Rule 3 in which the intersection of the alphabets consists of the collapsed communication event.

2.4. Integration

The translation rules can be considered as a set of functions from the trace-based domain to the PN domain: they achieve the translation of the trace sets according to the definitions and the laws of the CSP model. Rules 1 and 2 belong to the set of rules which translate the trace set of the individual sequential processes. Rules 3 to 5 are used to build the PN skeleton of the whole system through the composition of pairs of processes. Let P and Q be two processes. If they have an empty intersection, Rule 4 is directly applied to perform the composition. If they have a non empty intersection, and since in our method the composition must preserve the identities of the involved processes, the composition is achieved by applying Rules 3 and 4 as follows:

- Rule 3 is applied to obtain the common subnet;

- the equivalent PN representation of P and Q are joined over the resulting common subnet;

- a place and a transition corresponding to a dummy event are added to complete the composition of the processes according to the second point of Rule 4.

A *compound process* is the process resulting from the composition of two or more processes, and we use the * operator to denote the composition of two processes (P*Q). At most N-1 compositions of pairs of processes, primitive or compound, are needed for a system of N concurrent processes. In this way, the PN skeleton of the system results from a structured and systematic procedure, which enables the straightforward management of systems, even complex systems consisting of many processes. The integration step is exemplified in Section 3.

2.5. Adding external assumptions

As explained above in this phase the PN skeleton is completed by introducing the external assumptions which describe the dependencies of the state of a process (i.e. of a component) on the state of other processes. This means that the resulting PN skeleton models a subset of the traces described by the CSP processes since the external assumptions contribute to reduce the set of the feasible traces. At the current state of research we have identified the following four classes of constraints from which the external assumptions are derived:

- precedence constraints;

- resource contention constraints;

- inhibition constraints;

- constraints of non-deterministic behavior.

Precedence constraints correspond to external assumptions which define a precedence order on two events of two concurrent processes P and Q. In terms of Petri nets, this involves adding a place (interlock, see [7]) between the two events. An interlock can also be used to extend the model to the case of asynchronous communications. Indeed, they can be expressed by means of a precedence constraint between the send event and its related receive event. In this case the place represents a buffer in which the messages are stored.

Resource contention constraints correspond to external assumptions which define the rules on the concurrent access to shared resources. We focus on a simple case that can be described by critical regions. In terms of Petri nets, it involves adding a place modeling the critical region that has to be accessed in mutual exclusion by the processes.

Inhibition constraints correspond to external assumptions which define the restrictions on the evolution of a process P, depending on the current state of some other process Q. This is the class of constraints involving the concept of simultaneity or overlapping in time of the states. A common situation could be a requirement stating that an event of P cannot occur until Q has left state S. In terms of Petri nets, this situation is modeled by an inhibitor arc.

Non-deterministic communication constraints are introduced to cope with a common problem which arises modeling synchronous communications if a non-deterministic choice exists between a number of send or receive events. In this situation some sequences of events are not feasible since the occurrence of a send must have a corresponding receive event. In terms of Petri nets this problem is solved by causing the firing of a send transition to enabling only its related receive transition and disabling the other ones.

The PN figures related to the above mentioned cases are described in more detailed in [8].

2.6. Temporization

The previous phases allow to obtain a PN representation of the system in a rigorous and modular way, but the introduction of timing information into the model is a necessity for real-time embedded systems analysis. The temporization phase consists of building a quantitative model on the PN skeleton by extending the obtained standard PN net to include time and adding the proper timing parameters. This is done in two steps: a) by selecting a Timed Petri Net (TPN) class and modifing the PN skeleton according to its semantics; b) by defining the quantitative parameters on the net.

Many TPN classes have been proposed in literature. Usually time has been added to the Petri net model in three ways, namely by associating delays with transitions, places or tokens[1]. Our approach requires that time is related to events and so we use TPN classes in which time is associated to transitions.

There are different possibilities: either a fixed time interval is associated to each transition [11] or Min and Max times can be used to define a range of delays to each transition [9], or a random variable representing the firing delay can be considered, so yielding stochastic Petri Net (SPN). SPN with exponentially [2] distributed delays have been proved to be isomorphic to homogeneous Markov chains whereas deterministic firing delays make building a Markov or semi-Markov model more difficult [1].

The PN skeleton of the system can be easily transformed into a TPN skeleton belonging to any one of these classes by changing the necessary transitions in timed transitions. The details of the implementation of this step and the introduction of the timing parameters depend on the class selected, which best suits the problem. For example, if the GSPN class is selected, only the transitions corresponding to time consuming events are changed in timed transitions and probabilities related to immediate transitions representing the choice among different possibilities must be defined. Moreover, some transitions could be split into a sequence istantaneous transition-place-timed transition. This is the case of transitions in the PN skeleton modeling both synchronization and data exchanges between processes.

The markings of the states of the TPN skeleton reachability graph will be equal to or a subset of the markings of the PN skeleton. This is because of the additional restrictions imposed by the TPN class definition on the firing rules. In the next Section we will shown by means of the case study that this consequence of the temporization phase can have important implications in the analysis of a real-time system.

Once the TPN skeleton is obtained and the quantitative model is completed different metrics can be defined to perform the desired analysis. At this aim different techniques can be used as simulation, reachability graph analysis and Markovian analysis (where it is possible). The detailed description of the transformation of the PN skeleton into a timed PN model of the system is beyond the aims of this work. It is described in [8], [16] where the GSPN class has been considered.

3. Case study

Leveson and Stolzy [7] used Petri nets to model a railway crossing control system in order to conduct a safe state analysis. In this Section, we show how the proposed method is applied, starting from the same system requirements, in order to build the Petri net specification with our structured approach.

The system to be constructed is a controller for a gate at a railway crossing. The goal is to build a safe system, capable of ensuring that the train cannot be in the crossing while the gate is up. The requirements specify the interactions between the controller and the train (consequently between the controller and the gate) when the train approaches, enters and leaves the crossing. The application of the method is described step by step below, according to the phases presented in Section 2.

3.1. Informal system description

Three processes are clearly identified: a train (T), a control mechanism (C) that can be implemented both in hardware and software, a level crossing gate (P).
a) Events
The meaningful events for each process (specified in brackets) are the following:

E1. synchronization between the train and the control. The train signals its arrival to the control mechanism (T,C);

E2. synchronization between the train and the control. The train informs the control mechanism that it has crossed the gate (T,C);

E3. synchronization between the control mechanism and the gate. The control mechanism tells the gate to lower the barrier (C, P);

E4. synchronization between the control mechanism and the gate. The control mechanism tells the gate to raise the barrier (C,P);

E5. train passing (T);

E6. barrier down (P);

E7. barrier up (P).

  The processes are assumed to be non-terminating.
b) States
Definition of the states of each process:
train

TS1. the train is approaching the gate if there has not been any synchronization with the control mechanism yet (initial state);

TS2. the train is leaving if its second synchronization with the control mechanism has just taken place;

TS3. the train starts crossing if its first synchronization with the control mechanism has just taken place;

TS4. the train ends crossing if it has just passed.

control mechanism

CS1. the control mechanism is waiting for the approaching signal from the train if there has not been any synchronization with the train yet (initial state);

CS2. the control mechanism is receiving the leaving-signal from the train if the down-signal synchronization with the gate has just taken place;

CS3. the control mechanism is sending the down-signal to the gate if the first synchronization with the train has just taken place;

CS4. the control mechanism is sending the up-signal to the gate if the second synchronization with the train has just taken place;

CS5. the control mechanism is resetting if the up-signal synchronization with the gate has just taken place.

level gate

PS1. the gate is open if the barrier is up (initial state);

PS2. the gate is closed if the barrier is down;

12

PS3. the gate is <u>opening</u> if the up-signal from the control mechanism has just arrived;

PS4. the gate is <u>closing</u> if the down-signal from the control mechanism has just arrived.

c) Assumptions
In this simple example only internal assumptions on the states are necessary:
train

TA1. The train is in state TS2 iff the previous state was TS4;

TA2. The train is in state TS3 iff the previous state was TS1;

TA3. The train is in state TS4 iff the previous state was TS3.

control

CA1. The control mechanism is in state CS2 iff the previous state was CS3;

CA2. The control mechanism is in state CS3 iff the previous state was CS1;

CA3. The control mechanism is in state CS4 iff the previous state was CS2;

CA4. The control mechanism is in state CS5 iff the previous state was CS4.

level gate

PA1. The gate is in state PS2 iff the previous state was PS4;

PA2. The gate is in state PS3 iff the previous state was PS2;

PA3. The gate is in state PS4 iff the previous state was PS1;

PA4. The gate is in state PS1 iff the previous state was PS3.

d) Temporal specifications
Events E5, E6 and E7 are time-consuming. The timing parameters associated with such durations are denoted as Ttrans, Tdown and Tup, respectively. The remaining events are assumed to be instantaneous.

3.2. Definition of the trace-based specifications

Point a) of the informal description defines the alphabet of each process. A name is assigned to each event in list a):
    E1: sync1 E2: sync2 E3: sync3 E4: sync4 E5: crossing E6: down E7: up
    Notice that for brevity's sake we have already replaced the send and receive events with their related communication events, namely sync1, sync2, sync3, sync4. We assume that they initially had standard names so that the trace compiler is subsequently able to recognize them and apply Rule 5.
    The alphabets of the processes T,C,P are the following:
αT={sync1, sync2, crossing}

$\alpha C=\{$sync1, sync2, sync3, sync4$\}$

$\alpha P=\{$sync3, sync4, up, down$\}$ We have:

$\alpha T\cap\alpha C=\{$sync1,sync2$\}$, $\alpha C\cap\alpha P=\{$sync3,sync4$\}$, $\alpha T\cap\alpha P=\varnothing$

All processes are recursive since the informal description specifies that they are non-terminating.

Below we report the algebraic specification of each process according to the notation introduced in Section 2.

TS1, CS1, PS1 are the initial state of the processes T, C, P respectively. The definitions of such states are:

TS1: **approaching(t)**$\equiv<>$

CS1: **waiting(t)**$\equiv<>$

PS1 is also the end state of P (see PA4), so open(t) will be defined below. From point b) of the informal system description above, we derive the following:

TS2: **leaving(t)**$\equiv t'\in\{$sync2$\}$

TS3: **startcross(t)**$\equiv t'\in\{$sync1$\}$

TS4: **endcross(t)**$\equiv t'\in\{$crossing$\}$

CS2: **leavsig(t)**$\equiv t'\in\{$sync3$\}$

CS3: **downsig(t)**$\equiv t'\in\{$sync1$\}$

CS4: **upsig(t)**$\equiv t'\in\{$sync2$\}$

CS5: **reset(t)**$\equiv t'\in\{$sync4$\}$

PS1: **open(t)**$\vee t'\in\{$up$\}$

PS2: **close(t)**$\equiv t'\in\{$down$\}$

PS3: **opening(t)**$\equiv t'\in\{$sync4$\}$

PS4: **closing(t)**$\equiv t'\in\{$sync3$\}$

For this system, the internal assumptions simply define for each process a total ordering relation in its alphabet:

TA1: **PTsync2:** $t'\in\{$sync2$\}\Leftrightarrow$ **endcross(t'')**

TA2: **PTsync1:** $t'\in\{$sync1$\}\Leftrightarrow$ **approaching(t'')**

TA3: **PTcrossing:** $t'\in\{$crossing$\}\Leftrightarrow$ **startcross(t'')**

CA1: **PCsync3:** $t'\in\{$sync3$\}\Leftrightarrow$ **downsig(t'')**

CA2: **PCsync1:** $t'\in\{$sync1$\}\Leftrightarrow$ **waiting(t'')**

14

CA3: **PCsync2:** $t' \in \{sync2\} \Leftrightarrow$ **leavsig(*t*")**

CA4: **PCsync4:** $t' \in \{sync4\} \Leftrightarrow$ **upsig(*t*")**

PA1: **PPdown:** $t' \in \{down\} \Leftrightarrow$ **closing(*t*")**

PA3: **PPinit:** $t' \in \{sync3\} \Leftrightarrow$ **open(*t*")**

PA2: **PPend:** $t' \in \{sync4\} \Leftrightarrow$ **close(*t*")**

PA4: **PPup:** $t' \in \{up\} \Leftrightarrow$ **opening(*t*")**

Hence, these assumptions define the precedence constraints between events belonging to the same alphabet. It is now possible to generate the set of legal traces for each process:
traces(T)= $\{<>\} \cup \{< sync1, crossing, sync2 >\}*$
traces(C)= $\{<>\} \cup \{< sync1, sync3, sync2, sync4 >\}*$
traces(P)= $\{<>\} \cup \{< sync3, down, sync4, up >\}*$

3.3. Domain transformation

The traces of the three processes are translated into their equivalent PN subnets. In this example the sets of the traces consists of elementary recursive sequences. Figure 2a) shows the PN subnet obtained by applying the translation rules (Rule 1 and Rule 2) described in Section 2. Transitions are named as the events they represent and places as the related states whose names are derived from the underlined words in the informal description (list b)).

Notice that the transition modeling the cyclic closure of the subnet representing the process P has been replaced by the event up, since in this case the initial and the end state are the same (the gate is initially open as well as after the train has left). The next step requires integration of the subnets in order to build the PN skeleton of the system. The alphabets of T and P have an empty intersection; this means that the set traces(T|||P) consists of every interleaving between the traces of T and P, whereas the alphabets of T and C only have the communication events in common; the same holds for processes P and C.

3.4. Integration

Although the composition could be accomplished in two steps (joining process C and T and then obtaining (C*T)*P, it is more intuitive in this case to perform the integration in three steps:

1. composition of the train process T and control process C (T*C);

2. composition of the gate process P and control process C (P*C);

3. composition of T*C and P*C to obtain the PN skeleton of the system.

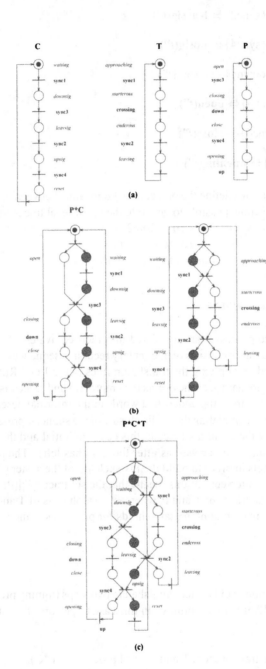

Figure 2. PN specification of the system

In our study all the precedence constraints between events are synchronous communications between processes. They reduce the number of possible interleaving of events. Hence the sets of traces of the compound processes are:

$$traces(T * C) = \{<>\} \cup \{< sync1, crossing, sync3, sync2 >\} * \cup$$
$$\{< sync1, sync3, crossing, sync2 >\} *$$

$$traces(P * C) = \{<>\} \cup \{< sync1, sync3, sync2, down, sync4, up >\} * \cup$$
$$\{< sync1, sync3, down, sync2, sync4, up >\} *$$

Notice that the elements of the pairs (crossing, sync3) and (sync2, down) are independent and can thus occur in any order. Figure 2b) shows the integrated subnets obtained by the trace compiler through the composition process described in the previous Section. The independence between the above mentioned events is expressed by the parallelism of the related transitions (Rule 4), whereas the synchronous communications are translated by means of Rule 5. As we have already explained above, the third composition which builds the PN skeleton of the system is obtained by integrating T*C and P*C over the common subprocess C. The intersection of the two PN subnets representing T*C and P*C is shaded in Figure 2b).

3.5. Adding external assumptions

In this case there are no constraints involving different processes, thus the final PN skeleton of the system is the output of the previous phase; it is shown in Figure 2c). The reachability graph of the net is shown in Figure 3 and the reachable markings are reported in Table 1, where the columns correspond to the places in Figure 2c) numbered from 1 to 13 in breadth-first order, starting from the first level (i.e. discarding the starting place at level 0). From an analysis of the reachability graph we can state that the system is not safe, because the markings M3 and M6 are high-risk states: in the first case the train has passed when the gate was open and in the second case when the gate was closing.

3.6. Temporization

The TPN class that best suits the problem is that introduced in [9] where fixed Min and Max delays are associated to each transition in the net. In fact the times involved in the problem are deterministic and we are not interested in the evaluation of some performance indices rather than in a safety analysis.

The high-risk states are shown to be avoidable by introducing the time in the net. One solution is to put a time constraint on the transitions *sync3*, *down* and *crossing* such that *down* could fire before *crossing*. Thus the minimum time delay associated to *crossing* (i.e. the time that the train takes to cover the distance from the gate) must be greater than the maximum time nedeed to the firing sequence *sync3*, *down*:

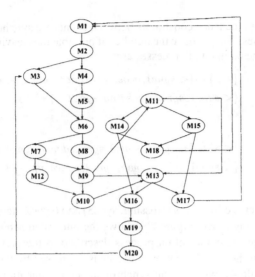

Figure 3. Reachability graph of the PN skeleton

Table 1. Reachable markings of the PN net in Figure 2c).

M1	1	1	1	0	0	0	0	0	0	0	0	0	0
M2	0	0	1	1	1	0	0	0	0	0	0	0	0
M3	0	0	1	0	1	1	0	0	0	0	0	0	0
M4	0	0	0	1	0	0	1	1	0	0	0	0	0
M5	0	0	0	1	0	0	1	0	0	0	1	0	0
M6	0	0	0	0	0	1	1	1	0	0	0	0	0
M7	0	0	0	0	0	0	0	1	1	1	0	0	0
M8	0	0	0	0	0	1	1	0	0	0	1	0	0
M9	0	0	0	0	0	0	0	0	1	1	1	0	0
M10	1	0	0	0	0	0	0	0	0	1	1	0	0
M11	0	0	0	0	0	0	0	0	1	0	0	1	1
M12	1	0	0	0	0	0	0	1	0	1	0	0	0
M13	1	0	0	0	0	0	0	0	0	0	0	1	1
M14	0	1	0	0	0	0	0	0	1	0	0	0	1
M15	0	0	1	0	0	0	0	0	1	0	0	1	0
M16	1	1	0	0	0	0	0	0	0	0	0	0	1
M17	1	0	1	0	0	0	0	0	0	0	0	1	0
M18	0	1	1	0	0	0	0	0	1	0	0	0	0
M19	0	0	0	1	1	0	0	0	0	0	0	0	1
M20	0	0	0	0	1	1	0	0	0	0	0	0	1

$$Min(crossing) > Max(sync3) + Max(down)$$

18

Since the closing rate of the barrier is obviously a fixed constant K, we have the following constraint:

$$Min(crossing) - Max(sync3) > K$$

This inequality mirrors the situation in the real system, where timing constraints will be imposed on the controller (*sync3*) and the train speed and/or train distance from the gate at the time of synchronization with the controller (*crossing*).

So this example shows how the real-time constraints imposed on the final TPN skeleton will ensure that the gate is closed before the train passing. Time introduction will reduce the reachability set by eliminating the risk states.

For this kind of safety critical embedded real-time systems, Leveson has also described run-time checks needed to detect critical timing failures [7].

4. Conclusions

In this paper we have presented a structured approach to the formal specification of concurrent systems, based on the transformation of a trace-based specification into a Petri net model. The transformation procedure from the complete trace-based specification to the Petri net domain is fully automatable.

Two alternative approaches to the event-based specification of concurrent systems are the constrained expressions method [3], and the method proposed by Sorensen et al. [13]. The constrained expression formalism is used to perform an algebraic analysis in order to determine whether a particular event, or sequence of events, appears in any possible system behavior. This is achieved by first describing the event sequences for each component process, and then removing those interleavings that represent illegal or impossible behaviors. Our method differs from this approach in that it is a specification technique that directly generates only the feasible traces of a process and aims to allow a more general system analysis.

The approach described in [13] builds a Markov model of the system starting from its specification as a CSP process. This method does not preserve the identities of the different system components and can be applied if its behavior is deterministic. The approach we have presented can be applied to the generation of a stochastic model of the system, provided that a stochastic PN class is used. Moreover it generates an executable representation of the system that is well suited to a structural analysis of its properties. The proposed method reduces the complexity of a hand-made construction of the formal model, by allowing a net representation of the whole system to be constructed from separate specifications of the behavior of each component (process), and of the interactions between them. The Petri net is used in the simulation and analysis steps. The method has been successfully applied in the specification and verification of a complex real-world, high-integrity system, namely an unmanned railway transportation system. The Petri model was used to analyze and validate the functional behavior of the systems under critical conditions.

Acknowledgments

This work has been supported in part by grants from CNR and MURST.

Notes

1. See [12] and [15] as examples of the last two cases.

References

1. Ajmone-Marsan, M., Chiola, G., "On Petri Nets with Deterministic and Exponential Transition Firing Times," Lecture Notes in Computer Science, Vol. 266 [24], 1987, pp. 132–145.
2. Ajmone-Marsan, M., Balbo, G., Chiola, G., Conte, G., Donatelli, S., Franceschinis, G., "An Introduction to Generalized Stochastic Petri Nets," Microelectronics and Reliability, 1991, pp. 699–725.
3. Avrunin, G.S., Dillon, L.K., Wileden, J.C., Riddle, W.E., "Constrained Expressions: Adding Analysis Capabilities to Design Methods for Concurrent Software Systems," IEEE Trans. on Soft. Eng., Vol. SE-12, Feb. 1986, pp. 278–292.
4. Donatelli, S., Franceschinis, G., Mazzocca, N., Russo S., "The EPOCA Integrated Environment Software Architecture," in G. Haring, G. Kotsis (Eds): Proc. of the 7th Int. Conf. on Modelling Techniques and Tools for Computer Performance Evaluation, Vienna, Austria, May 1994, Lecture Notes in Computer Science 794.
5. Hoare, C.A.R., "Communicating Sequential Processes," Prentice-Hall, Englewood Cliffs, NJ, 1985.
6. Jelly, I.E., "Directions in Software Engineering for Parallel Systems," Proc. of the 28th Hawaiian Conference on Systems Science, Hawaii, Jan. 1995, IEEE-CS Press.
7. Leveson, N.G., Stolzy, J.L., "Safety Analysis Using Petri Nets," IEEE Trans. on Soft. Eng., Vol. SE-13, No. 3, Mar. 1987, pp. 386–397.
8. Mazzeo, A., Mazzocca, N., Russo, S., Savy, C., Vittorini, V., "Formal specification of concurrent systems: a structured approach," submitted for publication to The Computer Journal.
9. Merlin, P.M., Farber, D.J., "Recoverability of Communication Protocols-Implications of a Theoretical Study," IEEE Trans. on Comm., Vol. COM-24, Sept. 1976.
10. Murata, T., "Petri Nets: Properties, Analysis and Applications," Proc. of the IEEE, Apr. 1989, pp. 541–580.
11. Ramamoorthy, C.V., Ho, G.S., "Performance Evaluation of Asynchronous Concurrent Systems Using Petri Nets," IEEE Trans. on Soft. Eng., Vol. 6, No. 5, Sept.1980.
12. Sifakis, J., "Use of Petri Net for Performance Evaluation," Proc. of the 3rd. Int. Workshop on Modeling and Performance Evaluation of Computer Systems, Amsterdam, 1977.
13. Sorensen, E.V., Nordahl, J., Hansen, N.H., "From CSP Models to Markov Models," IEEE Trans. on Soft. Eng., Vol. SE-19, No. 6, June 1993.
14. "UltraSAN User's Manual," Center for Reliable and High-Performance Computing; Coordinate Science Laboratory, University of Illinois at Urbana-Champaign.
15. Van der Aalst, W.M.P., Odijk, M.A., "Analysis of Railway Stations by Means of Interval Timed Coloured Petri Nets," Real Time Systems, Vol.9, No.3, Nov. 1995.
16. Vittorini, V., "An integrated algebraic-operational approach to the analysis of concurrent systems," Ph.D. Thesis, Dipartimento di Informatica e Sistemistica, Universita' di Napoli "Federico II", February 1995 (in Italian).

Real-Time Systems, 13, 237–251 (1997)

A Highly Dependable Computing Architecture for Safety-Critical Control Applications

BERND J. KRÄMER   bernd.kraemer@fernuni-hagen.de

NORBERT VÖLKER   norbert.voelker@fernuni-hagen.de

FernUniversität, Faculty of Electrical Engineering, D-58084 Hagen, Germany

Abstract. More and more technical systems are supervised, controlled and regulated by programmable electronic systems. The dependability of the entire system depends heavily on the safety of the embedded software. But the technological trend to entrust software with tasks of growing complexity and safety relevance conflicts with the lacking acceptance of rigorous proofs of software safety.

Based on an international standard for higher level programming languages for programmable logic controllers (PLC, IEC 1131-3), a mathematically based method for validating the behavioral correctness and the functional safety of graphical designs of safety-critical control applications is introduced. The design elements taken from a domain specific module library are proven correct and safe only once. The functional correctness and satisfaction of safety requirements of new application graphical programs can then be shown effectively by reference to the proven properties of the library components used. This approach is part of an comprehensive computing architecture for safety-critical control programs which is presented in a survey.

Keywords: safety-critical real-time systems, PLC programming, dependable software, modular verification, higher order logic theorem proving

1. Introduction

Programmable Electronic Systems are spreading to more and more fields of everyday life. They can be found in household appliances, motor vehicles of higher price ranges, emergency shut-down systems of nuclear power plants, medical treatment systems, traffic control systems, or process automation.

Severe accidents in the chemical and nuclear power industry, spectacular plane crashes and intrusions into company and government computer networks have increased the suspicion generally nursed in society that insufficient quality of the software embedded in these technical applications is the main cause of system unreliability. Thus, the technological trend to more flexible and complex systems and devices is opposed by the growing safety awareness of modern society and a critical attitude towards software taking over control in technical solutions. In addition, in Germany and other countries, technical devices and equipment that can endanger human life or the environment have to be licensed formally by regulatory authorities before being taken into use and later during their life-time.

These authorities are still quite reluctant licensing exclusively program controlled safety related automation systems. In general, no safety-critical systems containing software of non-trivial complexity are licensed, as yet, because: rigorous proof techniques and robust tools that can be used effectively by practitioners in regulatory authorities and in the application domain are not available; although existing design guidelines and testing procedures may help to prevent or detect design and programming errors, they cannot

21

guarantee the absence of faults that may cause a disaster; the method of diverse back-translation currently used by the TÜV Rheinland and other regulatory bodies is very time consuming and does not scale up. In this approach, the inspector tries to reconstruct a specification from the assembly or machine code manually and check it for conformity with the developer's specification. The method is effective in the sense that it is even able to detect compiler errors but experience has shown that it does not scale up. Up to two man-months are needed, for example, to verify four kByte of machine code.

1.1. Hardware versus Software Safety

Safety techniques of traditional engineering disciplines deal mainly with random failures of hardware. Design faults are not taken into consideration seriously because it assumed that they can be avoided by systematic design and validation techniques and because the extensive use of hardware components has demonstrated their dependability.

For hardware, this assumption is justified due to the relatively low system complexity and because a particular hardware design is typically produced in large quantities. These assumptions cannot be transferred to software intensive systems since software does not wear out, and programming faults are always systematic. The largest source of errors are design and specification faults, particularly non-considered situations, ambiguous or contradictory requirements.

In spite of some remarkable progress in the fields of standard software and libraries of re-usable software modules, the majority of today's program systems still represents individual solutions that have no extensive usage history. Moreover, software contains an extremely large, often even infinite number of discrete system states which in addition — in contrast to hardware — rarely are regular. This fact heavily reduces the possibilities to run exhaustive program tests or to create realistic test conditions.

1.2. Formal Methods

Experiences in other engineering disciplines suggest that mathematically based methods provide an adequate approach for precise specification, design, and quality assessment of dependable program systems. It is even expected that the use of formal methods for the construction and validation of certain safety-critical application classes will be required explicitly by legislature, as is already the case in the security domain [15]. Further evidence was collected recently during an international seminar entitled "Functional Safety of Program Controlled Electronic Systems" [4].

Unfortunately it must be realized that formal methods are hardly used in software practice. Few exceptions include the formal specification and verification of the emergency shutdown system of the Darlington reactor in Canada [14]; the use of formal methods systems in the development of IBM's CICS system in Great Britain [16]; or the extensive use of verification systems for military applications with strong data security requirements in the USA and Canada.

Reasons why many practitioners abstain from formal methods are certainly unrealistic expectations about the contribution of formal methods because people are often confusing correctness with adequacy. Establishing correctness means to compare two formal objects, e.g., a specification and a corresponding program, and answer the question: "Are we doing the thing right?". This is, what formal methods can help to achieve. Determining the adequacy of a specification, design, or a program, however, means to answer the question: "Are we doing the right thing?" by comparing the formal object's behavior with our mental expectations. Here, formal methods are of lesser help because they cannot guarantee that our understanding and model of the real world is appropriate. The accident of the Lufthansa plane caused by a design error in Warsaw for some years ago is an example for the fact that correct implementations of inappropriate software specifications[1] cannot be discovered by formal verification. Formal proof techniques can only verify mathematical objects like requirement, design or program specification concerning properties such as consistency, soundness and completeness. Another reason for disappointment results in the fact that many formal methods and their associated tools reach their limits as soon as they are applied to problems of a complexity usual in practice. Also the requirements for a formal basic training of the users of formal methods, which often are too high, form an acceptance threshold still being too high today.

1.3. Overview

This contribution describes methodological aspects of a high integrity systems project. We focus on the development and analysis of software for programmable logic controllers (PLC) with high safety requirements. The language concepts for PLC programming were defined in the international standard IEC 1131-3 [1]. They are especially suited for industrial automation projects which we chose as a focal application domain. The limited complexity of algorithms and dats structures used and the rich body of domain knowledge enables us to tailor suitable and mature formal methods to the work procedures of practitioners in the field.

In the following section, we outline the IEC languages relevant for our approach. Section 3 presents an overview of a safety-oriented computing architecture which is partly realized. In Section 4, we introduce a simple example along which we discuss the formal specification and verification of graphically designed application programs with recourse to already proven properties of their component modules taken from an application-specific library of standard building blocks. Finally, we discuss further work aiming at the completion of our high integrity systems development architecture.

2. Language Concepts of the IEC Standard

The standard IEC 1131-3 contains four compatible languages. The *Function Block Diagram (FBD)* and the *Sequential Function Chart (SFC)* languages have a visual representation, while *Structured Text (ST)* is a conventional higher level programming language with a textual syntax. Function block types are the central language elements of FBD. The standard includes a set of function block types realizing basic processing functions of process automation. Each function block type encapsulates a data structure which is divided into input, output and internal state variables of arbitrary types. Output variables are functionally dependent on the input and state variables. Outputs and inputs of function block instances can be "wired together" to a diagram of function blocks forming the actual application program.

Fig. 1 shows a hierarchical function block type, called measure, which is built up from an instance of the standard type IN_A, named input, and two instances of the standard type SAM, named highlimit and lowlimit. IN_A converts an analogue value read from address HWADR to a numerical value. This value is output at port X after having been scaled to the boundary values available at the ports XMIN and XMAX. The unit of the measured value is determined by the character string provided at input t XUNIT. Function block type SAM serves as a boundary value switch for the value at the X port. It also enables the storage of alarms or messages. Signal X is compared with the boundary value which arrives at port S. The Boolean value LOW determines whether S is interpreted as an upper or a lower bound. In the former case, the Boolean output QS switches from 0 to 1 in case S is exceeded and returns to 0 in case the value at port X drops under S-SHYS. Similarly, when LOW is 1, the Boolean output QS switches from 0 to 1 once the value at port X drops below the value at port S and returns to 0 when it exceeds S+SHYS again. SHYS describes the switching difference or hysteresis. Port SHYS may remain unconnected and is then assumed to be 0.

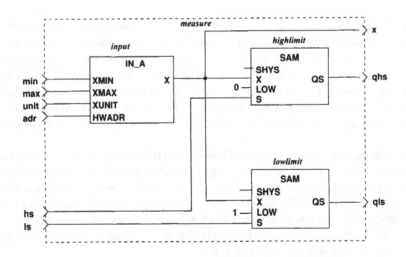

Figure 1. Derived function block type measure

In fig. 2 the interface definition or signature of SAM is described in ST. ST is a block structured language which mainly follows Pascal concerning notation and language concepts. In addition, it offers a task concept to handle parallel real-time processes. Apart from being defined by graphical composition using the FBD language, the behavior of a hierarchical function block type can also be determined by an ST program. The program

text then occurs as a function block *body* between the interface declaration and the keyword
END_FUNCTION_BLOCK.

```
FUNCTION_BLOCK SAM

   VAR_INPUT          (* input declarations *)
      X: NUM;         (* input value *)
      LOW: BOOL;      (* type of boundary value *)
      S: NUM;         (* boundary value *)
      SHYS: NUM :=0   (* hysteresis of the boundary value S *)
   END_VAR;

   VAR_OUT
      QS: BOOL        (* boundary value infringed *)
   END_VAR;

body

END_FUNCTION_BLOCK
```

Figure 2. Signature of function block type SAM

   The second graphical process control language of the standard, SFC, can be regarded as an
industrial application of Petri nets. The language concepts in SFC include transitions, steps
and actions. They serve to co-ordinate the processing of function block instances which are
regarded as asynchronous sequential processes. Fig. 6b shows an example with four steps
s0 to s3. The transitions separating these steps are enabled by Boolean conditions such as
lmax and tmax, by preceding steps, and by the actions *fill*, *heat* and *discharge* associated
with steps s1, s2, and s3, respectively. The double framed box states that s0 is the initial
state.

3. A Safety Oriented Computer Architecture

Different possibilities for the formal specification and verification of standard and application specific function modules serving as library elements have been demonstrated in
previous work. A first prototype design and validation environment tailored to the graphical notation of higher PLC languages was introduced in [8]. Similar to the approach in [6],
algebraic data structuring concepts were used for requirement specification. The properties
of elementary function modules are verified with the help of structural induction techniques
supported by term rewrite systems. For the analysis of the dynamic behavior of entire
function block diagrams, higher Petri nets marked with instances of abstract data types
were suggested. In [10] the components of an emergency shut-down system used in reactor
control were specified in higher order predicate logic and verified mechanically using the
Isabelle/HOL theorem proof assistant.

Figure 3. Structure of a safety oriented computing architecture

The suggested specification, design and validation method is supported by the computing architecture presented in fig. 3. The architecture includes ergonomically designed tools, a library of re-usable software modules as well as a simple specialized run-time environment. The latter is tailored for the language concepts of the standard and runs on a fault tolerant hardware (cf. [6]). Two prototype versions of the hardware architecture are operational. They are supported by a simple runtime environment. It was designed to serve the needs of the IEC standard and reduce the potential for introducing errors.

A customized computer supported process model organizes the entire development and licensing process. It leads application developers in companies and engineers affiliated with regulatory authorities through the prescribed process steps. In addition, it executes clerical development steps automatically and records the entire construction and licensing process. The essential components of the development process have been described in [9]. An executable refinement of this process model can be designed for concrete application domains and work procedures with reasonable expenditure. The basic idea is to formulate the individual steps of an application specific development or licensing process as production rules [11].

Relying on the standard IEC 1131-3, a joint commission of the German Associations of Engineers (VDI) and Electrical Engineers (VDE) jointly produced the design guideline VDI/VDE 3696 [2]. This guideline provides a basis for the planning and configuration of process control systems. It supplies a vendor independent description language and a collection of standard function module definitions. As a preliminary work for the construction of an application specific module library, the module specifications named in the guideline design were investigated in [17]. Throughout this study

- incomplete information about the algorithmic definition of certain function modules such as time components, standard PID regulators, or characteristic components, were discovered and lacking information was added;

- ambiguities, contradictions, redundancies and design flaws in individual module descriptions were identified and recommendations for their removal were developed;

- a large number of module definitions was formally verified.

The approach to construct application programs by re-use of library components reduces development time and effort. In combination with the use of formal methods, it also provides the basis for effective formal verification and validation of critical properties of new applications because we can rely on proven properties of the modules involved. It is a desired side effect of this approach that the costs for the verification of library modules can thus be shared among many applications.

4. Verification of Hierarchical Function Modules

Our main approach to verification is based on higher order logic (HOL) theorem proving [13]. This means that both specifications and implementations are modeled in a very powerful, general purpose logic. The correctness of an implementation then becomes a mathematical theorem which can be proven using standard mathematical reasoning. Since all proofs are checked by the Isabelle/HOL system, we can be very confident that no invalid deductions occur during the proof process.

Our computation model is based on the cyclic execution of reactive systems [12]. Controllers are described essentially as net-lists of function blocks. Function blocks are entities which have their own private memory that persists from one invocation to the next. In accordance with guideline VDI/VDE 3696, the only form of communication between function blocks is the passing of parameters from output to input ports. Therefore the evaluation order of function blocks within one cycle does not matter as long as causal dependencies between function blocks are respected. Such dependencies exist if a function block A provides input for another function block B. Therefore, the execution of A must be completed before that of B is started. Currently, we are restricting ourselves to single tasks. Hence we do not need to address issues such as scheduling or processing of interrupts.

The underlying processing model contains two principal components (see Fig. 4)

- a plant, also called "unit under control", and

- the controller.

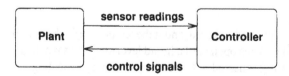

Figure 4. Control process model

In every cycle, the current reading of a number of plant sensors are digitized and communicated to the controller. After a certain delay, the controller responds by sending control signals back to the plant. The state of the plant is modeled via a number of real-valued variables. Its behavior will usually be given as a set of linear differential equations. Our approach does not require that the behavior of the plant is deterministic. Instead, it is sufficient to have a number of inequalities which limit the maximal possible variation of the plant variables per cycle.

Upper bounds for the delay in the response of the controller can be calculated by summing up upper bounds for the individual delays caused by the execution of each activated function block. In general, these delays depend on the current inputs and states of the function blocks. However, in practice, it is usually both possible and sufficient to give constant upper bounds for the delays of all components and thus also for the whole controller.

Qualitative time behavior is expressed by Linear time Temporal Logic (LTL) formulas (cf. e.g. [12]). Timers are treated as nondeterministic functions subject to the condition that the values of subsequent readings increase monotonously as long as there is no reset. Of course, we also assume that the readings of timers are compatible with the bounds on the function block delays. We believe that this simple model of time is adequate for most control applications.

The reactive model sketched above allows modular verification. Thus, base components can be verified first. In subsequent steps, these results can be used in the proof of the correctness of the entire control system. In this inductive process requirements specifications of base components are combined by logical conjunction, while a composite program is formed by identifying input and output variables of connected components according to their wiring in the given diagram.

For the mechanical support of the proof method, we are working on an extension of a method for the verification of elementary function blocks which already has been implemented with the help of the proof system Isabelle/HOL [10].

4.1. Example

As a simple example, we consider the process control for a container automation taken from VDI/VDE guideline 3696. The physical configuration is depicted in fig. 5. In the VDI/VDE guideline the automation task for this example is described informally as follows [2]:

> If a start button is pressed and held, and if the temperature is below 40° C, the filling valve opens and remains open until a liquid level of 90 % is reached. Subsequently, the container casing is heated with steam by opening the heating valve until 90° C are reached. Now, the emptying valve is opened until the filling height has fallen below 5 %; then the control goes back to its initial step and the whole process is repeated.

The controller for this system depicted in fig. 6a is composed of two instances of function block measure, which was shown in fig. 1a, and an instance of function block sequence, whose structure is illustrated in fig. 6b.

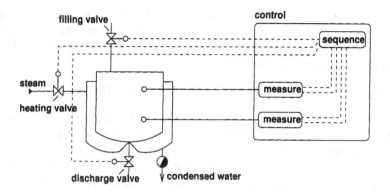

Figure 5. Automatic Level and Temperature Control

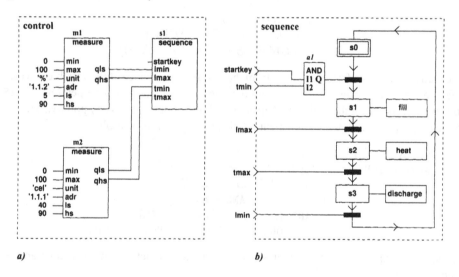

Figure 6. Function block sequence

4.2. Specification of Function Blocks

The core of the control system shown in fig. 6a is function block sequence. It has five Boolean inputs *startkey, tmin, tmax, lmin, lmax* and controls the three actions *fill, heat,* and *discharge.* The control algorithm is specified through an SFC with four steps s0, s1, s2, and s3. These steps are sequentially dependent on each other so that exactly one of them can be activated at any time.

As mentioned before, our approach to formal verification is based on higher order logic theorem proving. For modeling the behavior of function blocks, we have adopted the relational approach advocated in [13]. A function block with n input and m output ports is represented by an $(n + m)$-ary relation on streams. Every stream parameter refers to the flow of values communicated through the corresponding port. For example, the HOL type of the standard function block SAM is

$$\text{SAM} :: \text{NUM STREAM} \times \text{SIGNAL} \times \text{NUM STREAM} \times \text{NUM STREAM} \times \text{SIGNAL} \rightarrow \text{BOOL}$$

where SIGNAL is an abbreviation for BOOL STREAM. As this typing suggests, the identification of function block ports in the HOL representation is by order of parameters and not by name. Streams of some type a are simply modeled as functions from type NAT to a. As usual in HOL, function application is denoted simply by juxtaposition, i.e. $QS\,n$ is the value of the stream QS at time step n. The relation between the values of input and output parameters of SAM is characterized by:

$$
\begin{aligned}
\text{SAM } &X\ LOW\ S\ SHYS\ QS\ = \\
\forall n.\ \ QS\,n\ =\ (\ \ &LOW\,n \wedge X\,n < S\,n \\
\vee\ \ &\neg(LOW\,n) \wedge S\,n < X\,n \\
\vee\ \ &0 < n \wedge QS\,(\text{pred } n) \\
&\wedge\ (LOW\,n \wedge X\,n \le S\,n + SHYS\,n \\
&\quad \vee \neg LOW\,n \wedge S\,n - SHYS\,n \le X\,n))
\end{aligned}
$$

The readability of this formula suffers from the frequent occurrence of the variable n which refers to the current point of time. Using the linear time temporal logic operator ALWAYS and stream versions of the logical and arithmetical operations obtained by pointwise lifting (cf., e.g., [12]), the following equivalent specification of SAM is possible:

$$
\begin{aligned}
\text{SAM } &X\ LOW\ S\ SHYS\ QS\ = \\
\text{ALWAYS }(QS\ &\text{Eq}\ (\ \ LOW\ \text{AND}\ X\ \text{Less}\ S \\
&\text{OR}\ \text{Not}\ LOW\ \text{AND}\ S\ \text{Less}\ X \\
&\text{OR}\ (\lambda n.0 < n)\ \text{AND}\ \text{Pre}\ QS \\
&\quad \text{AND}\ (LOW\ \text{AND}\ X\ \text{Le}\ S + SHYS \\
&\qquad \text{OR}\ \text{Not}\ LOW\ \text{AND}\ S - SHYS\ \text{Le}\ X)))
\end{aligned}
$$

As usual, the expression $\lambda n.E$ denotes a λ-binding, i.e. a function with formal parameter n and result E.

Using an embedding of the SFC formalism in HOL, a third equivalent formulation of SAM via sequential function charts would also be possible. Instead, we will give below some temporal logic formulas which can be derived from the SFC specification of the function block type sequence in fig. 6b. These formulas all assume the premise

    sequence *startkey lmin lmax tmin tmax fill heat discharge*

where

$$\text{sequence} :: \text{SIGNAL} \times \ldots \times \text{SIGNAL} \rightarrow \text{BOOL}$$

is the relation on input- and output signals derived from the SFC specification. Further, the stream

```
Step :: (STEP SET) STREAM
```

consists of the corresponding set of activated steps of sequence over time.

First, the possible sets of active steps of sequence are characterized by the formula:

$$\text{ALWAYS } (\text{Step} =_c \{s_0\} \text{ OR Step} =_c \{s_1\} \text{ OR Step} =_c \{s_2\} \text{ OR Step} =_c \{s_3\})$$

where the operator

$$=_c :: a \text{ STREAM} \times a \rightarrow \text{SIGNAL}$$

compares the values of a stream with a constant:

$$\forall n.\, (x =_c a)\, n \;=\; (x\, n = a)$$

Because the steps $s_0, \ldots, s_3$ are pairwise different, the formula above implies that always exactly one of the four steps is active.

In the following, we will drop the outer ALWAYS quantifier in LTL formulas and assume an implicit universal quantification over all instances. The LTL formulation of the step transition relation of the SFC specification of function block sequence can be derived directly by symbolic evaluation of the specification:

$$
\begin{aligned}
\text{Step} =_c \{s_0\} &\implies \text{NEXT (UNLESS } (\textit{tmin} \text{ AND } \textit{startkey})\ (\text{Step} =_c \{s_0\})) \\
\text{Step} =_c \{s_1\} &\implies \text{NEXT (UNLESS } \textit{lmax}\ (\text{Step} =_c \{s_1\})) \\
\text{Step} =_c \{s_2\} &\implies \text{NEXT (UNLESS } \textit{tmax}\ (\text{Step} =_c \{s_2\})) \\
\text{Step} =_c \{s_3\} &\implies \text{NEXT (UNLESS } \textit{lmin}\ (\text{Step} =_c \{s_3\})) \\
\text{Step} =_c \{s_0\} \text{ AND NEXT } (\textit{tmin} \text{ AND } \textit{startkey}) &\implies \text{NEXT (Step} =_c \{s_1\}) \\
\text{Step} =_c \{s_1\} \text{ AND NEXT } \textit{lmax} &\implies \text{NEXT (Step} =_c \{s_2\}) \\
\text{Step} =_c \{s_2\} \text{ AND NEXT } \textit{tmax} &\implies \text{NEXT (Step} =_c \{s_3\}) \\
\text{Step} =_c \{s_3\} \text{ AND NEXT } \textit{lmin} &\implies \text{NEXT (Step} =_c \{s_0\})
\end{aligned}
$$

The temporal operator UNLESS P Q is valid at some point in time, provided Q remains TRUE as long as P is FALSE. It does not say anything about the truth of P. The NEXT operator shifts a stream by one instance "to the left":

$$\forall n.\, (\text{NEXT } x)\, n \;=\; x(n+1)$$

The initial state and the correspondence between steps and actions complete our list of propositions about the function block sequence:

$$
\begin{aligned}
\text{Step } 0 &= \{s_0\} \\
\textit{fill} &= (\textit{Step} =_c \{s_1\}) \\
\textit{heat} &= (\textit{Step} =_c \{s_2\}) \\
\textit{discharge} &= (\textit{Step} =_c \{s_3\})
\end{aligned}
$$

Composition and instantiation of function blocks lead to analogous operations on relations. Ports which connect components inside a function block can be made invisible to the outside by existential quantification. Assuming a relation measure modeling the function block of the same name, the net-list description of control in fig. 6a can be specified as follows:

> control *startkey fill heat discharge* ==
> $\exists$ *m1.qls m1.qhs m2.qls m2.qhs s1.lmin s1.lmax s1.tmin s1.tmax* .
> measure 0 100 '%' '1.1.2' 5 90 *m1.qls m1.qhs* $\wedge$
> measure 0 100 '*cel*' '1.1.1' 40 90 *m2.qls m2.qhs* $\wedge$
> sequence *startkey s1.lmin s1.lmax s1.tmin s1.tmax fill heat discharge*
> $\wedge$ *m1.qls* = *s1.lmin* $\wedge$ *m1.qhs* = *s1.lmax*
> $\wedge$ *m2.qls* = *s1.tmin* $\wedge$ *m2.qhs* = *s1.tmax*

Following our process model of fig. 4, the function block control receives analogue input streams from the plant at the addresses '1.1.1' and '1.1.2'. The controller responds by sending the Boolean signals *fill, heat, discharge* to the plant.

4.3. Verification of a Safety Property

As we have already seen in the previous section, some safety properties can be derived from the individual specifications of the involved function alone. For example, the specification of function block type sequence implied immediately that no more than one of the three actions *fill, heat* and *discharge* can be activated at any time.

As an example for a safety property of the composed system, we will give an informal sketch of the derivation of an upper bound for the liquid level in the tank. For this, we assume that the current value of the liquid level is read with a frequency of $f = 100 Hz$. The maximal flow of liquid into the tank is dfmax = 2% per second. Further, we assume that the filling valve reacts with a mechanical delay of dvalve = 0.5 s, i.e. it takes this time for the filling valve to open and close completely after the corresponding change of the controller signal *fill*. During the opening or closing of the valve, we assume a linear increase and decrease of the liquid stream, respectively.

In order to obtain an upper bound for the delay in the controller response, we examine the tasks accomplished by the components. In addition to one analog-digital conversion, these consist mainly of a couple of simple arithmetic and Boolean operations. Since none of the programs implementing a function block requires a loop or a backward jump, upper bounds for the execution times can be obtained by simply multiplying the number of instructions with the maximal execution time per instruction. We will require in the following that the controller delay is less than dctrl = 1*ms*. Considering the small number of instructions necessary for implementing the function blocks, this delay could even be achieved easily with a slow, low-cost PLC and a program written in a strictly sequential, higher level programming language.

For the following verification, we assume a composition of control as in fig. 6a. This is expressed by the predicate

> control *startkey fill heat discharge*

where the relation control is defined as above. Further we assume that

$$m1.qls \quad m1.qhs \quad m1.X \quad s1.lmin \quad s1.lmax$$

denote the respective streams at the input/output ports of function block $m1$ and $s1$. Thus, ignoring rounding errors in the digitization step, the last reading of the fluid level in the container is given by the value of the stream $m1.X$.

Recall that our aim is to obtain an upper bound on the liquid level in the tank. Assuming that the tank is initially empty, i.e.

$$(m1.X)\,0 < m1.ls$$

we deduce from the specification of SAM

$$(m1.qls)\,0 = \text{TRUE}$$

The equality

$$m1.qls = s1.lmin$$

reflects the composition of these two ports in control. Using it, we obtain

$$(s1.lmin)\,0 = \text{TRUE}$$

Next note that the water level can not rise while the controller is in step $s0$:

$$(x = m1.X \text{ AND } \text{Step} = \{s0\}) \implies \text{NEXT}\,(m1.X \leq x)$$

This implies

$$\text{Step} = \{s0\} \implies s1.lmin$$

by induction over the number of instances and using the precondition of the only transition which leads to an activation of step $s0$.

The increase in the liquid level is always bound by dfmax

$$\begin{aligned}(x = m1.X) &\implies \text{NEXT}\,(m1.X \leq x + \text{dfmax}/f) \\ &= \text{NEXT}\,(m1.X \leq x + 0.02\%)\end{aligned}$$

The switching from step s1 to s2 takes place as soon as $m1.X$ exceeds $m1.hs$. Because of the last two inequalities, simple arithmetic shows that the value of $m1.X$ in this instance must be less than $m1.X + \text{dfmax}/f$. Due to the controller delay, the filling will continue for another $1ms$, leading to a maximal intake of $\text{dfmax} * \text{dctrl} = 0.002\%$. Integration shows that during the closing phase of the filling valve, the liquid level will rise by at most

$$\int_0^{0.5} (2 - 4 * t)\%\, dt = 0.5\%$$

Since no more liquid is added to the tank in the remaining steps of the control loop, induction over the number of instances proves

$$\begin{aligned}\forall t.\ \text{level}(t) &< m1.hs + \text{dfmax}/f + \text{dfmax} * \text{dctrl} + 0.5\% \\ &= 90.522\%\end{aligned}$$

5. Further Work

The results presented in the main body of this paper are supplemented by an ongoing "Study of programming languages with limited features suitable for control applications with safety tasks" supported by the Federal Institute of Labor. This study aims at

- identifying language elements and constructions of higher programming languages which may cause design faults, impede a sufficient analysis of the program code, or render the formal proof of functional correctness, safety and timing constraints difficult or even impossible;

- selecting reliable subsets of suitable programming languages staggered according to safety requirement classes;

- characterizing corresponding restrictions for syntax and type checkers, compilers, and run-time environments for the chosen languages;

- designing comprehensive methods for systematic programming and formal verification of safety-oriented program systems.

Starting-point for this study are the Safe Technical Language defined by Daimler-Benz AG [5], the comparative evaluation of programming languages for real time applications presented in [7], and our own preliminary work.

In parallel, an international project is planned in which, for the first time, a complete real-time operating system kernel shall be specified and verified formally.

Theorem prover based verification methods such as the one sketched above are very trustworthy, flexible and support modular proofs. However, in general they require a so-phisticated guidance by the user. Hence it is very important to find ways to automates recurring development steps. In this respect, the integration of automatic model check-ing procedures such as pioneered by N. Shankar for the PVS system seems particularly promising.

Another and for the automation practice decisive step is finally the construction of a complete development environment. According to this approach, it should support a math-ematically precise description of safety-critical components of PLC-based process control systems and the verification of fulfilling the given safety requirements with the help of formal proof techniques. An ergonomic design of the construction and proof processes and tools matching the working processes in development laboratories and licensing authorities such as Technical Supervising Organizations and internal company quality control groups must be focused here. However, this step can only be executed sensibly in close co-operation with interested vendors, users and evaluators for PLC controllers in safety-critical fields, who we are still looking for.

Acknowledgments

The authors would like to thank R. Lichtenecker and the anonymous referees for their helpful comments on an earlier version of the paper.

Notes

1. The software prevented the pilots to switch the reverse thrust on in time. The reason was that the control software failed to detect the plane's touching of the ground due to the reduced friction caused by rain and the undercarriage's one-sided touching of the ground caused by severe side winds.

References

1. IEC Draft International Standard 1131-3. *Programmable Controllers. Part 3: Programming Languages.* International Electro-technical Commission, Geneva, 1992.
2. VDI/VDE Richtlinie 3696. Herstellerneutrale Konfigurierung von Prozeßleitsystemem. Technical report, Düsseldorf, 1993 (in German).
3. R.M. Cardell-Oliver and C. Southon. A Theorem Proving Abstraction of Model Checking. Technical Report CSM-253, Department of Computer Science, University of Essex, England, 1995.
4. W.J. Cullyer, W.A. Halang, and B.J. Krämer (Eds.). High integrity programmable electronic systems. Dagstuhl-Seminar-Report 107, IBFI GmbH, Schloß Dagstuhl, D-66687 Wadern, Germany, 1995.
5. G. Egger, A. Fett, and P. Pepper. Formal specification of a safe PLC language and its compiler. Technical report, Daimler-Benz AG, 1994.
6. W.A. Halang, S.-K. Jung, B.J. Krämer, and J. Scheepstra. *An Safety Licensable Computing Architecture.* World Scientific, 1993.
7. W.A. Halang and A.D. Stoyenko. Extending PEARL for industrial real-time applications. *IEEE Software,* 10(4):65–74, 1993.
8. W.A. Halang and B.J. Krämer. Achieving high integrity of process control software by graphical design and formal verification. *Software Engineering Journal.* 7(1):53–64, January 1992.
9. W.A. Halang and B.J. Krämer. Safety assurance in process control. *IEEE Software,* Special issue on Safety-Critical Software:61–67, January 1994.
10. W.A. Halang, B.J. Krämer, and N. Völker. Formally verified building blocks in functional logic diagrams for emergency shutdown system design. *High Integrity Systems,* 1995.
11. B.J. Krämer and B. Dinler. Software process environment drives hardware synthesis. In P.A. Ng, F.G. Sobrinho, C.V. Ramamorthy, R.T. Yeh, and L.C. Seifert, editors, *Systems Integration '94,* volume 1, pages 354–361, Sao Paulo, Brazil, 1994. IEEE Computer Society Press.
12. Z. Manna and A. Pnueli. *The Temporal Logic of Reactive and Concurrent Systems,* volume 1. Specification. Springer Verlag, 1992.
13. T.F. Melham. *Higher Order Logic and Hardware Verification.* Cambridge University Press, 1993.
14. D.L. Parnas, J. van Schouwen, and S.P. Kwan. Evaluation of safety-critical software. *Communications of the ACM,* 33(6):636–648, 1990.
15. H. Pohl and G. Weck (Eds.). Internationale Sicherheitskriterien, Oldenbourg Verlag, München, Wien, 1993 (in German)
16. J. Wordsworth. Practical experience of formal specification: A programming interface for communications. In C. Ghezzi and J.A. McDermid, editors, *ESEC '89 2nd European Software Engineering Conference,* number 387 in Lecture Notes in Computer Science, pages 140–158, Berlin, Heidelberg, New York, 1989. Springer Verlag.
17. G. Wulf. Überprüfung des Richtlinienentwurfs VDI/VDE 3696 und Verifikation der darin definierten Funktionsbausteine. Diplomarbeit, FernUniversität, 1995 (in German).

Real-Time Systems, 13, 253–275 (1997)

The ProCoS Approach to Correct Systems

HANS LANGMAACK   hl@informatik.uni-kiel.d400.de
Institut für Informatik und Praktische Mathematik, Christian-Albrechts-Universität zu Kiel, Preusserstr. 1-9, D-24105 Kiel, Germany

Abstract. ProCoS is the name of the ESPRIT project "Provably Correct Systems". A system is seen as a technological system with embedded controlling processors, sensors, actuators, connecting channels and timers in a physical environment, especially a real-time or hybrid system with digital and continuous components. The goal of ProCoS is to contribute to mathematical foundation for analysis and synthesis and to mathematical principles, techniques and tools for systematic and correct design and construction of systems, especially in safety-critical applications.

The article discusses the notion of system correctness and explains its non-absolute nature. Two forerunners of ProCoS are described, the so-called stack of Computational Logic Inc., Austin, Texas, and the three views of concurrent processes – nets, terms and formulas – of E.-R. Olderog. ProCoS is going beyond the forerunners and has extended the description levels: Requirements and systems architectural language, specification language, high-level programming language, machine language, hardware description language and description language for asynchronuous circuits.

A major achievement of ProCoS is to have related the semantic models of several different system development levels and to have shown up how to mathematically prove correct the transitions between these levels w.r.t. the semantic relations. The Duration Calculus gives a basis for semantics and verification and crosses the boundary between discrete and continuous models.

The lecture has been given at the Dagstuhl-Seminar "High Integrity Programmable Electronic Systems", 27. 02. - 03. 03. 95, organized by W. J. Cullyer, W. A. Halang and B. J. Krämer.

Keywords: computer-based real-time systems, safety-critical applications, requirements, systems architecture, specification, high-level timed programming, machine programming, hardware description, asynchronous circuits, correctness, duration calculus

1. Introduction

ProCoS is the name of the European ESPRIT Basic Research project 7071. The name stands for "Provably Correct Systems". Participants are University of Oxford (C. A. R. Hoare, coordinator), Danish Technical University Lyngby (A. P. Ravn), University of Oldenburg (E.-R. Olderog) and University of Kiel (H. Langmaack) [6], [26], [4], [25].

A system as investigated by ProCoS is a technical system with embedded controlling processors, sensors, actuators, connecting channels, timers in a physical environment, especially a real-time system (hybrid system) with explicit parallelism and lower and upper time bounds to guarantee maximal and minimal operating rates for hard real-time problems.

The goal of ProCoS is to contribute to mathematical foundation for analysis and synthesis and to mathematical principles, techniques and tools for systematic and correct design and construction of systems, especially of safety-critical systems where failures may result in heavy dangers.

The project's approach is constructive and proof oriented, as opposed to test oriented. Drastic reductions of failure risks are expected. Systematic proving is expensive, but it seems rewarding, at least for safety-critical systems. Where rational reasoning makes sense and is possible it should be done in order to achieve logical mathematical certainty. Logics and mathematics are the only sciences where one can find undeniable insights in infinite collections of elements, e.g. by induction principles. Informatics needs substantial knowledge in problems about infinities.

In the light of Engineering of Computer Based Systems ECBS (a discipline developing between informatics and classical engineering sciences) ProCoS systems are *control* systems rather than *information processing* systems. In the former, a variety of sensor and actuator types (e.g. A/D and D/A converters) have to be handled, whereas in the latter case interfaces are mainly with people through monitor screens and keyboards. Nevertheless, information processing systems are important in ProCoS in the form of correctly proved tools like programming language translators, operating systems, theorem provers and proof assistants. Incorrect development tools, with their resulting incorrect machine programs and incorrect construction plans, severely compromise good designs on higher levels.

An ideal goal of ProCoS is *correctness*, e.g. of all binary machine programs and all hardware plans in the form of binary gate array net-lists which have been generated and are executed is depending only on trusted hardware and on rigorous mathematical reasoning. Trusted means that the hardware is assumed to function as described in manuals. The informatics idea of correctness and its proof is not restricted to software development. The idea can be extended to the engineer's whole construction process including physical system environment and material processor hardware. ProCoS shows how reasoning by proof calculi is possible even with control systems which are hybrid, which have not only digital components controlled by programmed processors but also continuous components, the actions of which are subjected to real number analysis with differential and integral equations.

2. Correctness

There is no absolute notion of correctness for systems or software. Correctness means satisfaction of required, demanded, actually defined properties. System components are abstract (immaterial, written on paper) or concrete (material). Abstract components are edifices of thought like theory of numbers, plans and designs like circuit and VLSI-designs, constructions like software and systems architecture. Concrete components are processor hardware, channels, sensors, actuators, timers, plant parts and physical environment. Correctness is only associated with abstract system parts. Their properties are of rational nature and therefore subjectable to logical-mathematical proof conductions.

High system dependability does not only demand correctness of the immaterial parts, it also requires adequate modeling of the physical parts and environment. Dependable working of information processing systems is relying very heavily on correctness; most of their serious failures are caused by faults of thought, not by spontaneously changing physical corpuscels. If ultra-high system dependability shall be guaranteed no better help is to be seen than to mathematically verify plans and software. See the articles of M.-C. Gaudel and of B. Littlewood, L. Strigini in the Predictably Dependable Computing Systems PDCS proceedings [11],[27], [37].

That correctness is non-absolute can best be seen e. g. with different reasonable correctness notions known for sequential programs π. We have syntactical notions like *syntactical correctness* (with respect to a *grammar*) and *static-semantical correctness*. The latter notion means a program fulfills *context conditions* or is a so called *proper program* with an associated *dynamic semantics*. More important are semantic correctness notions like *partial* or *total correctness* with respect to a *precondition* P_π and *postcondition* Q_π which obviously make sense only for proper programs. The user can and must make his decision among the parameters for correctness such that his purposes are served.

These different correctness notions evoke further different and delicate correctness notions if $\pi = trans$ denotes programming language *translation (compilation)* of source language *SL* to target (machine) language *TL*.

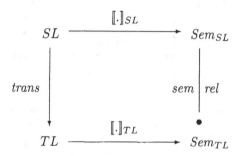

Regular termination and consequently total correctness of *trans* often cannot be achieved, e.g. if *trans* is the semantics of a binary coded translator program π^h_{trans} implemented on a real *host* computer with its restricted machine resources. So, in general, partial (not total) correctness of *trans* is a reasonable goal. The associated precondition P_{trans} gets specialized saying that source programs π_s are supposed to be proper ones. Appropriate postconditions Q_{trans} for *trans* will be discussed in connection with project language levels of ProCoS and its forerunner projects; Q_{trans} expresses reasonable semantic relation

$$[\![\pi_s]\!]_{SL} \; \frac{sem}{rel} \; \bullet \; [\![\pi_t]\!]_{TL}$$

between the semantics of source programs π_s and of target programs π_t.

The vast majority of compiler verification literature is only concerned with correctness of mathematically specified translation functions *trans* from *abstract* source programs π^a_s to target programs π^a_t for idealized languages and machines. This mathematical question and treatment of *translation specification verification* has to be contrasted to *translator implementation verification* where *trans* is implemented as a host language program π^h_{trans} for a host machine M_{HL} such that π^a_s and π^a_t must be represented as concrete data π^h_s and π^h_t of the host language. Translator implementation verification calls for mathematically sound software engineering methods and gets especially laborious if the host language *HL* is the binary code of a real processor. *Full translator verification*, i. e. specification plus implementation verification, will also be discussed more closely later.

3. Origins of the ProCoS-Idea

The ProCoS–idea is patterned after two forerunners. One is the so-called *stack* of Computational Logic Inc., Austin, (CLInc for short):

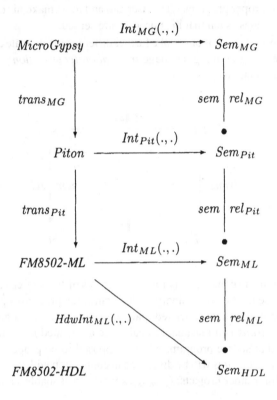

This consists of a stack-like model of four description levels [48]: High level *Pascal*-like programming language *MicroGypsy* [47], assembly language *Piton* [29], machine language *FM8502-ML* and a hardware register transfer description *HDL* of the processor *FM8502* in form of recursive functions for all hardware subcomponents [20].

CLInc's idea is to give full justification of all translations from high level programming languages down to hardware descriptions by correctness proofs conducted by the automated *Boyer-Moore-Theorem-Prover*. Translations *trans* and interpreters *Int* (semantics) are expressed in *Boyer-Moore-Lisp*-dialect and correctness postconditions Q_{trans} in quantifier-free first order so-called *computational logic*. Q_{trans} says that the state transformations $[\![\pi_s]\!]_{SL} = Int_{SL}(\pi_s, .)$ and $[\![trans(\pi_s)]\!]_{TL} = Int_{TL}(trans(\pi_s), .)$ together with representation *repr* and retrieving *retr* (abstraction) form a *communative diagram*.

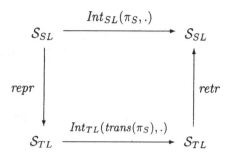

There are several reasonable notions of commutativity. For $trans_{MG}$ *bisimulation* actually can be proved, but for $trans_{Pit}$ only *upward simulation* is valid since the processor's running is limited by resource bounds. Nevertheless, the overwhelming majority of users with their discrete sequential problems is served quite well by upward simulation, because they can be sure that due source program executions are never deceived by employing a machine and by translation of source programs to target machine code: If a starting state $\sigma_s \in S_{SL}$ is representable and if $Int_{TL}(trans(\pi),\ repr\ (\sigma_s))$ is regularly terminating with final state σ_t' then source program interpretation $Int_{SL}(\pi\ ,\ \sigma_s)$ is also regularly terminating with final state $\sigma_s'\ =\ retr\ (\sigma_t')$, i. e. the machine calculated result σ_t' is well related to the source program result σ_s' . For the lowest part in CLInc's stack-diagramm let us only mention that Int_{ML} means machine code interpretation based on integer operations $+, -, *$, etc. whereas $HdwInt_{ML}$ means a more hardware gates-like interpretation based on Boolean operations $\wedge, \vee, nand$ etc..

Translator implementation correctness and thus full translator correctness is not treated in the CLInc-stack project. J S. Moore states that explicitly [29] and stresses the absolute necessity of implementation verification. The *Boyer-Moore System* is implemented in *Common Lisp* for which there is no full translator verification up to now. So CLInc's translation specification verification logically depends on the assumed availability of a trusted *Common-Lisp*-machine or -implementation.

The other ProCoS-forerunner is E.-R.Olderog's habilitation thesis 1989 "Nets, Terms and Formulas: Three Views of Concurrent Processes and their Relationship" [35]. Again, we see a stack-like model:

$$S \xrightarrow{\quad R^*_{Spec} \quad} R^*_{Spec}[\![S]\!]$$

$$|||\qquad\qquad\qquad ||$$

$$\pi \xrightarrow{\quad R^{**} \quad} R^{**}[\![\pi]\!]$$

$$N\Big\downarrow\qquad\qquad\qquad ||$$

$$N[\![\pi]\!] \xrightarrow{\quad R^* \quad} R^*(N[\![\pi]\!])$$

Hardware and machines are represented as safe Petri-nets [39] and high level programs by *CSP*-like process terms [18]. These two lower levels have a structure as in the CLInc stack: N is a translation of process terms into nets, R^* is an operational readiness semantics of nets, R^{**} is a denotational readiness semantics of process terms and the semantic relation boiles down to equality $=$.

As in good software engineering E.-R. Olderog puts a specification level with logical formulas S about observable communication traces above the program (term) level [36]. The transition relation $\equiv$ between specifications S and process terms π is generated by transformation rules. Specifications have a readiness semantics R^*_{Spec} as well, and the semantic relation is again equality $=$.

E.-R. Olderog shows correctnesses of $\equiv$ and N in a mathematical style. Transition from specifications down to machines is interrupted in a characteristic way: Translation N of processes π is effective-recursive whereas correctness demonstration $\pi \equiv S$ needs intuition. A calculus for $\equiv$ is semidecidable at best.

4.   The ProCoS Tower

ProCoS is going beyond the forerunners und has extended the description levels, especially by a requirements and systems architectural language *RL* in order to design hybrid automating systems [16].

1. Requirements and systems architectural language *RL* [38]. It is a time interval logic, a duration logic, allowing to speak about system states varying in time [49]. *RL* has a *duration calculus DC* which helps to derive valid duration formulas what may be supported by mechanical proof assistants like *PVS* [44]. *RL*-specifications can easily be embedded in J.R.Abrial's *Z* notation [45].

2. The specification language *SL* which is an elaboration of Olderog's trace logic. *SL* bridges the state oriented world of *RL* and the event oriented world of the *occam*-like [21] higher programming language *TimedPL*. *SL*-specifications consist of regular

expressions about observable event traces, of communication specifications in form of action systems, and of time constraints [40].

3. Higher programming language *TimedPL*. Like *occam*, *TimedPL* is designed for describing parallel processes. Lower time bounds can be prescribed as in occam [21]. *TimedPL* extends *occam* [31]: Upper time bounds can be prescribed to guarantee minimal operation rates, and timer and input guards in alternatives can be programmed. Time is spent in communications only, usual sequential statements do not take time. This is for the comfort of the user, clever translation has to hide time used by compiled machine instructions in succeeding communications [10], [33].

4. Machine Language *ML*. The binary *RISC*-code of the *transputer* of Inmos is the target code [22]. The ProCoS idea is to use realistic, not idealized machines and languages. Idealizations make proofs easier, but they leave full correct transition towards reality unclear. Every *transputer* can be coupled to neighboring *transputers* by four input and four output channels and thus can work as part of an asynchronously operating parallel computer net.

5. Hardware description language *HDL*. "Programs" consist of netlists for field programmable gate arrays. ProCoS translates *TimedPL* not only into *ML* but also directly into *HDL* [17].

6. Description language for asynchronous circuits *AHDL*. Switching circuits are effectively compiled and implemented in CMOS-circuitry with sectionwise continuously acting physical components. Duration Calculus gives a basis for verification and crosses the boundary between discrete and continuous models of switching circuits unlike most work on hardware verification [8, 50, 24].

As for the forerunner projects, the ProCoS tower mirrors the stages of the simplest system development model, the waterfall model. ProCoS is a prototype project and so it is not recommendable to study more evolved development models.

5. Duration Logic

Duration Calculus *DC* has proved to be a convenient instrument to treat semantics universally across all development stages. To the outside observer and user a hybrid system shows up as a collection of *state components*

$$s_i : \mathcal{R}^+ \longrightarrow \mathcal{R}$$

varying in *time* $= \mathcal{R}^+$, the non-negative real numbers. Arithmetic and logic operators allow to form *state expressions se* which yield derived values on the s_i for *time points*. In case values are only 1 (=*true*) or 0 (=*false*) we speak about *state predicates* or *formulas P*.

Important properties of the s_i often better show up as properties of *time intervals* $I = [b, e]$ than of time points t . So we form *elementary duration terms*

$$\int se : \mathcal{I}(\mathcal{R}^+) \to \mathcal{R}$$

which associate $\int_b^e se\, dt$, the integral value, to every interval $I = [b, e]$. $\int P$ yields exactly that duration at which P in I holds, and $l =_{Df} \int 1$ yields the length of a given I. As above, arithmetic and logic operators allow to form *non-elementary duration terms* or even *duration formulas* D with values 0 or 1 only. Such formulas D we want to use in *RL* for hybrid system descriptions and D expresses whether or not D *holds* for a given interval.

Important Examples:

$$\lceil \rceil \Leftrightarrow_{Df} l = 0$$ length of a given I is 0

$$\lceil P \rceil \Leftrightarrow_{Df} \int P = l \wedge l > 0$$ length of a given I is > 0 and P holds nearly everywhere in I

$$true \Leftrightarrow_{Df} 1$$ *true* holds for every I

$$false \Leftrightarrow_{Df} 0$$ *false* holds for no I

$$D_1 ; D_2$$ a given $I = [b, e]$ may be chopped into $I_1 = [b, m]$, $I_2 = [m, e]$ such that D_1 holds for I_1 and D_2 for I_1

$$\Diamond D \Leftrightarrow_{Df} true; D; true$$ there is a subinterval of I where D holds

$$\Box D \Leftrightarrow_{Df} \neg \Diamond \neg D$$ D holds for any subinterval of I

$$D \longrightarrow \lceil P \rceil \Leftrightarrow_{Df} \neg \Diamond (D ; \lceil \neg P \rceil)$$ D leads to $\lceil P \rceil$. Or: Every subinterval T of I with D is followed by one with $\lceil P \rceil$ (in case T leaves room in I)

$$D \xrightarrow{t} \lceil P \rceil \Leftrightarrow_{Df} D \wedge I = t \to \lceil P \rceil$$ t sec long D leads to $\lceil P \rceil$

$$D \xrightarrow{\leq t} \lceil P \rceil \Leftrightarrow_{Df} D \wedge I \leq t \to \lceil P \rceil$$ t sec or less long D leads to $\lceil P \rceil$

We say D is *holding generally* or *from beginning on* if D is holding for all $[0, e] \subset \mathcal{R}^+$.

6.   Case Study Gas Burner and Closer Description of the ProCoS Tower

Development of a gas burner shows the ProCoS development stages.

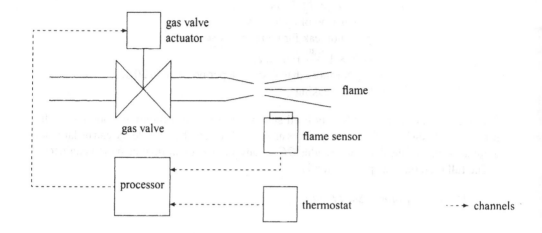

6.1.   Requirements Capture and Systems Architecting

6.1.1.   Requirements Capture

We have three elementary state predicates to formulate the user's functional and safety requirements R:

$$Flame \quad \text{for} \quad \text{flame is burning,}$$
$$Gas \quad \text{for} \quad \text{gas is streaming,}$$
$$Heatreq \quad \text{for} \quad \text{heat is requested.}$$

We may form the composed state formula

$$Leak \Leftrightarrow_{Df} Gas \wedge \neg Flame$$

We have two functional requirements. Stop burning:

$$Stop \Leftrightarrow_{Df} \lceil \neg Heatreq \rceil \xrightarrow{40} \lceil \neg Flame \rceil$$
$$\text{40 sec no heatrequest leads to no flame}$$

Start burning:

$$Start \Leftrightarrow_{Df} \lceil Heatreq \rceil \xrightarrow{40} \lceil Flame \rceil$$
$$\text{40 sec heatrequest leads to flame burning}$$

We have one safety requirement, safety from explosion:

$Safe \iff_{Df} \square((l \le 30) \Rightarrow (\int Leak \le 4)),$
in every period of up to 30 sec
gas must not leak for more than 4 sec
$\iff \int Leak > 4 \xrightarrow{\le 30} \lceil \neg Leak \rceil$
leaking for more than 4 sec in a period of up to 30 sec
leads to no leaking.

The latter equivalence holds only if all state predicates are sectionwise continuous. Its proof needs knowledge from real numbers analysis. Much of that knowledge can be laid into axiomatic rules of the duration calculus DC, a convenience to informaticians and engineers.

The full requirement specification is

$R \iff_{Df} Stop \wedge Start \wedge Safe$.

6.1.2. Natural Laws and Engineer's Assured Assumptions

What natural laws and engineer's assured assumptions A do we need beside system controlling design D to implement requirement R? Implementation means implication

$D \Longrightarrow (A \Longrightarrow R).$

For stop burning: Flame cannot burn without gas (natural law)

$NoFlame \iff_{Df} \lceil \neg Gas \rceil \xrightarrow{1} \lceil \neg Flame \rceil$

For start burning: Ignition mechanism works reasonably (engineer's assumption)

$Gasok \iff_{Df} \lceil Gas \rceil \xrightarrow{0.75} \lceil Flame \rceil.$

For safety: Just extinguished flame is stable for a while (natural law)

$NoFlicker \iff_{Df} (\lceil Flame \rceil; \lceil \neg Flame \rceil) \xrightarrow{\le 0.5} \lceil \neg Flame \rceil.$

The full set of assumptions is

$A \iff_{Df} NoFlame \wedge Gasok \wedge NoFlicker.$

6.1.3. Refinement towards Architecture

System controlling design D needs sensors and actuators. The state predicates *Heatreq*, *Flame* and *Gas* cannot immediately be observed in channel wires connected to the controller. So we have three further elementary state predicates *hr* , *fl* and *gas*. They are related to the thermostat and flame sensors (analog-digital converters) and to the gas valve actuator (digital-analog converter) by the following characteristic properties (*sa* indicates system architecture)

$$D_{sa} \Leftrightarrow_{Df} \lceil Heatreq \rceil \xrightarrow{\varepsilon} \lceil hr \rceil \wedge \lceil \neg Heatreq \rceil \xrightarrow{\varepsilon} \lceil \neg hr \rceil \wedge$$
$$\lceil Flame \rceil \xrightarrow{\varepsilon} \lceil fl \rceil \wedge \lceil \neg Flame \rceil \xrightarrow{\varepsilon} \lceil \neg fl \rceil \wedge$$
$$\lceil gas \rceil \xrightarrow{\varepsilon} \lceil Gas \rceil \wedge \lceil \neg gas \rceil \xrightarrow{\varepsilon} \lceil \neg Gas \rceil.$$

ε with $0 < \varepsilon < \frac{1}{9}$ is a time delay constant which hides that all elementary state predicates are approximations of reality.

6.1.4. Design of a Control Processor

Essential idea is that a controlling processor is going through phases. So we introduce a new state component

$$phases \mid \mathcal{R}^+ \Longrightarrow \{Idle, Purge, Ignite, Burn \}$$

with four derived state predicates *idle, purge, ignite* and *burn*:

$$idle \Leftrightarrow_{Df} phases = Idle, \ ...$$

The design conditions consist of initialization

$$Init \ 0 \Leftrightarrow_{Df} \lceil \ \rceil \vee \lceil idle \wedge \neg hr \wedge \neg fl \wedge \neg gas \rceil \ ; true \ ,$$

sequencing of phases

$$Seq \ 0 \Leftrightarrow_{Df} \lceil idle \rceil \longrightarrow \lceil idle \vee purge \rceil \wedge \cdots \ ,$$

progress of phases

$$Prog \ 0 \Leftrightarrow_{Df} \lceil idle \wedge hr \rceil \xrightarrow{\varepsilon} \lceil \neg idle \rceil \lceil$$
$$\lceil purge \rceil \xrightarrow{30} \lceil \neg purge \rceil \wedge \cdots \ ,$$

stability of phases

$$Stab \ 0 \Leftrightarrow_{Df} \lceil \neg idle \rceil \ ; \lceil idle \wedge \neg hr \rceil \longrightarrow \lceil idle \rceil \wedge$$
$$\lceil \neg purge \rceil \ ; \lceil purge \rceil \xrightarrow{\leq 30 - \varepsilon} \lceil purge \rceil \wedge \cdots \ ,$$

and synchronization of gas valve actuator

$$Syn \ 0 \Leftrightarrow_{Df} \lceil idle \wedge burn \rceil \xrightarrow{\varepsilon} \lceil \neg gas \rceil \wedge \cdots \ .$$

The conjuncted design conditions D_0 together with D_{sa} implement the requirements R w.r.t. the assumptions A

$$D_0 \wedge D_{sa} \Longrightarrow (A \Longrightarrow R).$$

This can be proved by mechanical reasoning in duration calculus DC [38, 44]. It is essentially the purge phase which implies the desired safety.

6.2. Correct Specification of the Control Processor

Design D_0 recommends to employ, beside timers for 1 sec and 30 sec, essentially three control processes: Heat, flame and main controller. The first two control thermostat resp. flame sensor, the latter one controls both the phases and the gas valve actuator. A problem is that semantics, i.e. observed behaviors, of *occam-* or *TimedPL*-processes are defined to be sets of timed communication event traces. In order to relate such processes to state-oriented designs event properties must be expressed by duration formulas.

Any piecewise continuous state predicate defines a *timed communication event trace*, namely state changes. So e. g. *hr* is associated with successive events *HeatOn* and *HeatOff*, *fl* with *Flon* and *Floff*, and *gas* with *GasOn* and *GasOff*. Heat and main controller together communicate *hon, hoff, tellheat* and *flfail*, flame and main controller communicate *flon, floff* and *tellfl*, $timer_n$ and main controller communicate set_n and $tick_n$ for $n = 1$ resp. 30.

We can visualize the architectural aspect described by the three controller components, by the timers and the connecting communication channels as shown in figure 1.

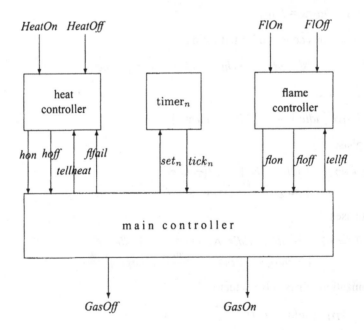

Figure 1. Architectural design of the three controller components

Design D_0 suggests a main controller loop of events (specifiable by a regular expression):

in initial *idle* phase:	hon .
in *purge* phase:	set_{30} . $tick_{30}$.
in *ignite* phase:	$GasOn$. set_1 . $tick_1$.
in *burn* phase:	$(tellheat . hon . tellfl . flon)^*$.
	$(tellheat . hoff$
	$\vee\ tellheat . hon . tellfl . floff . flfail)$.
again in *idle* phase:	$GasOn$. hon .
again in *purge* phase:	set_{30} . $tick_{30}$.
$\vdots$	$\vdots$

In order to satisfy time bounds imposed by the requirements for *purge* and *ignite* there are delays of 30 sec resp. 1 sec implemented by timers. One might think that an alternative like

$(hoff \vee\ floff)$.

might fully suffice for the *burn* phase, but that would lead to output guards in alternative statements (processes) for the heat resp. flame controller *TimedPL* programs. Such language constructs cannot be implemented on the real *transputer*. So we have to use a polling loop construction in the trace specification above and in the main controller *TimedPL* program later.

In general, a process specification of ProCoS' specification language *SL* has not only a *trace part* with regular expressions

TRACE *re*

for communication channel traces (context clearifies when *SL* means specification language resp. source language). We may specify further constraints on communication traces by a *state part* with *communication assertions*

COM	*ch*		
READ	$var_1, \cdots, var_m$	**WRITE**	$var^1, \cdots, var^n$
WHEN	enable-predicate (precondition) on non-changing read-variable values var_i and initial write-variable values var^j	**THEN**	effect-predicate (post-condition) on non-changing read-variable values var_i, initial and final write-variable values var^j resp. $var^{j'}$ and communicated value @ *ch*. (prime' is taken from J.R. Abrial's Z notation [45]).

as we know them from action systems (the gas burner needs not any state part). Furtheron, we have a *timing part* which specifies when channels are ready for communication. Lower and upper time bounds are expressed by

AFTER *re* **WAIT** (ch , t)   and   **AFTER** *re* **READY** (ch , t)

Time bounds have actual effects, provided such communications are not forbidden by trace and communication assertions. Unspecified time bounds mean $t = 0$ (in the gas burner example only timers need timing specifications).

Process specifications have interface parts where the involved channels and variables are named together with their type properties. Every channel is given an allowed *latency time* > 0 with the intended meaning; as soon as both partner processes are ready to communicate on a channel communication will take place within the specified latency time and especially ensure progress (unspecified latency means infinite latency).

As a small example with timing specifications we show $timer_n$ specification:

SPEC $timer_n$
   INPUT OF *signal* set_n **LAT** ε
   OUTPUT OF *signal* $tick_n$ **LAT** ε
   TRACE pref (set_n . $tick_n$)*
   AFTER (set_n . $tick_n$)*. set_n **WAIT** ($tick_n$, $n - \varepsilon$)
   AFTER (set_n . $tick_n$)*. set_n **READY** ($tick_n$, n)
END

M. Schenke and E.-R. Olderog [41] have developed general derivation rules which prove that the five conjuncted specifications heat-, flame- and main-controller, $timer_1$ and $timer_{30}$ implement design D_0.

6.3.   Correct High Level Programming of Control Process Components

Further correctly proved derivation or implementation rules in [41] and [33] lead from *SL* specifications to high level *TimedPL* programs, e.g. for the main controller in *occam*-like syntax:

   SYSTEM main-controller
      CHANNEL OF *integer*
         Gas, fl, flfail, hon, hoff, tellheat, tellfl
      VAR OF *integer*
         dummy, on, off
      VAR OF *Boolean*
         exit
      SEQ
         on : $= 1$
         off : $= 0$
         WHILE *true*
            SEQ
               | *hon* ? *dummy* | $\leq \lambda_1$
               | **DELAY** 30.0 | $\leq \lambda_2$
               | *Gas* ! *on* | $\leq \lambda_2$

$| \textbf{DELAY } 1.0 | \leq \lambda_2$
$| tellheat ! \ 0 | \leq \lambda_1$
$exit := false$
$\textbf{WHILE } \neg \ exit$
$\quad \textbf{ALT } \lambda_1$
$\qquad hon ? \ dummy$
$\qquad \quad \textbf{SEQ}$
$\qquad\qquad | tellfl ! \ 0 | \leq \lambda_1$
$\qquad\qquad | fl ? \ dummy | \leq \lambda_1$
$\qquad\qquad \textbf{IF } dummy = on$
$\qquad\qquad\quad | tellheat ! \ 0 | \leq \lambda_1$
$\qquad\qquad\quad \textbf{SEQ}$
$\qquad\qquad\qquad | flfail ! \ 0 | \leq \lambda_1$
$\qquad\qquad\qquad | Gas ! \ off | \leq \lambda_2$
$\qquad\qquad\qquad exit := true$
$\qquad hoff ? \ dummy$
$\qquad \quad \textbf{SEQ}$
$\qquad\qquad | Gas ! \ off | \leq \lambda_2$
$\qquad\qquad exit := true$

The two *signal* channels *GasOn, GasOff* are multiplexed in one *integer* channel *Gas* in order to avoid more than four output channels for the real *transputer*. λ_1 and λ_2 stand for real numbers as upper time bounds. Implementability of *SL*-specifications by *TimedPL*-programs requires proper choices for the gas burner, e. g. $0 < \lambda_1 < \frac{\varepsilon}{5}$ and $0 < \lambda_2 < \frac{\varepsilon}{2}$ where ε is from the architecture specification D_{sa} in chapter 6.1.3. $| \ statement \ | \leq \lambda$ expresses and requires that the sums of all communication latencies per execution path are bounded by λ sec. $\textbf{ALT } \tilde{\lambda}$ demands that the latencies of all associated input and timer guards (here *hon ? dummy* and *hoff ? dummy*) are bounded by $\tilde{\lambda}$ sec. Sequential language constructs in *TimedPL* do not take any time, a great comfort to the programmer.

6.4.   Correct Translation of *TimedPL* Programs to Machine Language *ML* Programs

6.4.1.   Translation Specification Verification

In section 3, in connection with CLInc's stack project we have pointed out that *information processing* users with their discrete sequential source programs are served quite well by the translation correctness notion of upword simulation. But the situation in ProCoS with its time-critical *process automatization* is different. Translation must guarantee liveness and regular termination of target machine programs if source programs have these properties. Here correct translation means *downward simulation* of source programs π by machine programs m what can be expressed by algebraic inequations between processes (compare second diagram in section 3):

$\pi \sqsubseteq repr \ ; \ m \ ; retr$ or equivalently $retr \ ; \ \pi \sqsubseteq m \ ; retr$.

(*retr*, *repr*) is a so called *simulation pair* with *retr* ; *repr* $\sqsubseteq Id$ and $Id \sqsubseteq repr$; *retr* where *Id* is the identity process and the right hand processes are said to be *better than*, to be *more deterministic than*, to *refine* or to *implement* the left hand ones. A simulation pair induces a *Galois connection* (F, G) between a more abstract and a more concrete process level with $F(\pi) \sqsubseteq m$ if and only if $\pi \sqsubseteq G(m)$.

Special care must be devoted to translation of timing conditions. Upper time bounds in *TimedPL* programs may be seen as allowed communication latencies of which are to be contrasted to hardware channel latencies of which the compiler developer and compiler program should have prior knowledge. Since usual sequential language constructs in *TimedPL* are assumed to take no time both hardware latencies and execution times of preceding compiled machine instructions must be hidden in allowed latencies. Although there are different sources of delays (and inaccuracies of our knowledge about them) in the execution of the target processor, e.g. *drift* and *granularity* of the hardware clock, *latency* of communications by protocols and *active time* spent for code execution, we believe we can safely subsume all effects under just one concept, the contribution of a process to its *communications' latencies*.

ProCoS' idea is to give correctness proof advice to realistic, not idealized engineering problems. Such attitude leads to large amounts of proof work and enforces to search for modularization techniques:

1. ProCoS has figured out algebraic laws on process implementation $\pi_1 \sqsubseteq \pi_2$ and process equality $\pi_1 = \pi_2$, and translation correctness theorems are proved for all source language constructs by successive algebraic calculations based on those laws [33] the justification of which is done in a separate proof level 3..

2. Algebraic technique has shown to allow successful automatic proving with the *OBJ3*-term rewriting system and the *PVS* verification system [7]. There is hope that the implemented proof strategies do work out even if source and target languages are modified and enlarged. This fact promises good support to industrial applications.

3. M. Müller-Olm has established a semantic model, a *predicate transformer semantics*, for the *process language* mentioned above in 1. and has proved the laws to hold [34]. ProCoS cultivates the idea and usage of a process language in the habit of a mathematician when he writes down terms and formulas which directly denote mathematical objects without employment of any semantics operators (brackets)which make difference of syntax and semantics explicit, but make proofs clumsier. Involved source and target programming languages may be immediately seen as sublanguages of the process language if syntactic flourishes are neglected.

M. Müller-Olm further modularizes translation verification in 1. by stepwise derivations of increasingly more abstract models of *transputer* execution. The Inmos instruction manual [22] presents only a semiformal model of the *transputer* execution cycle, there is no notion of a machine program nor of any machine language semantics. So M. Müller-Olm proposes six semantic process levels $L_1, \cdots, L_6$ with Galois connections (F_i, G_i)

$$L_{i-1} \overset{G_i}{\underset{F_i}{\rightleftarrows}} L_i$$

above base level L_0 where the *transputer* is seen as a process $M \in L_0$ consisting of all execution paths allowed by the manual's conditions for instructions.

In principle the G_i are families of abstraction mappings each parameterized by a machine program m (a base *RISC* instruction sequence with a symbolic execution start point) and by reserved parts of the *transputer's* memory for program storage and data workspace. In each abstraction step G_i one aspect of machine program execution can be treated in isolation:

L_1 : Symbolic view of control flow by hidden instruction pointer, no overwriting of program storage.

L_2 : Assembly language view with large *CISC* instructions and operands by hidden operand register.

L_3 : Relative data addressing view by hidden workspace pointer, workspace separated from program storage, no overwriting of memory outside workspace.

L_4 : Symbolic assembly language view with symbolic addressing of workspace words through variables in a symbol table.

L_5 : Forgetting all *transputer* registers and auxiliary variables for intermediate results.

L_6 : Forgetting all source program variables, only channel variable names remain visible.

L_4 , L_5 and L_6 are the appropriate levels to define correct *TimedPL* expression, statement and program translation and to prove *translation theorems* for the different source language constructs. The collection of translation theorems yields an implicit inductive definition of a translation function *trans* which can easily and correctly reformulated as a translator program π^h_{trans} in host languages *HL* like *StandardML* or *CommonLisp* with their recursive function procedure mechanisms and their appropriate rich data structures to represent source, target and possibly intermediate programs. M. Müller-Olm has constructed a *TimedPL* compiler in *StandardML*. Binary *transputer* codes for main-, heat- and flame-controler can be seen in [32].

6.4.2. *Translator Implementation Verification and Full Translator Verification*

We see from section 6.4.1 that the full translator verification problem for *TimedPL* reduces to the full translator verification problem of another high level language, now of a host language *HL* with discrete sequential translator programs without timing nor parallel subprocesses nor mutual communications. ProCoS pursues translation specification verification for *HL* (in fact *SubLisp* and *ComLisp*, functional and imperative sublanguages of *CommonLisp*) along the same lines as indicated for *TimedPL* in chapter 6.4.1 with the characteristic difference that upward simulation is relevant for *HL*. If the same target machine, e.g. the *transputer*, is used many proofs remain valid.

Nevertheless, no systematic and repeatable engineering techniques are known which truly warrant translator implementation correctness (and hence full translator correctness) with mathematical certainty for realistic source languages and existing target and host machines down to the bit level including assemblers, loaders, linkers, readers, printers and run time support programs. Standard software engineering theory is recommending stepwise application of refinement rules for machine implementations of mathematical functions like $trans$ or of high level host programs like π^h_{trans} [2]. Assume proved correct rules are available. Then, if unverified tools are employed they should be used only like typing assistants because, in general, the influence of unverified tools on rule applications is hardly controllable. Following slavishly the recommendation above, the compiler builder and verifier finally will have developed the whole compiler implementation by hand down to binary machine code and, hopefully, he will have meticulously checked each rule application. It is exactly this stadium where severe doubts in trustworthiness of the proceeding are emerging, too many slips are possible. Realistic perfect compiler construction and implementation is recommended to go a different way.

One idea to achieve compiler implementation correctness is to apply *bootstrapping*, i. e. to do translation verification for *HL* and to write a correctly developed *HL* to *ML* translator program π^h_{trans} in *HL* itself. Proved bootstrapping correctness guarantees: For full translator correctness it suffices that this single *HL* program π^h_{trans} can be correctly implemented in target machine code *ML*. Twofold translations of π^h_{trans} by an existing *HL* or *superHL* compiler and by the generated *HL* compiler yield an *HL* compiler "$trans(\pi^h_{trans})$" in *ML*. Since up to now no realistic compiler is fully verified we cannot be sure that "$trans(\pi^h_{trans})$" is truly correct; therefore our quotation marks. We can do the well known strong test translation of "$trans(\pi^h_{trans})$" by the *HL* compiler "$trans(\pi^h_{trans})$" on target machine M, but even a successfull test does not grant mathematical cercainty (successfull real tests have in fact been done with a prototype *ComLisp* compiler on the *transputer* processor).

We have seen in section 6.4.1 that translation correctness for realistic languages and processors should be proved in a modularized style by stepping through different target processor abstraction or, in reversed view, source language concretion levels where each one is treating specific language-processor aspects. This can be refined in a sequence of successive intermediate language translation passes $trans_i$ without additional translation verification expenditures. Whereas a direct mathematical inspection of the whole output "$trans(\pi^h_{trans})$" (generated by an executable *superHL* compiler) is not enough trustworthy, such inspection gets realistic if we execute $trans$ in well chosen portions so that source and generated target programs are in close structural neighbourship. This mathematical inspection resembles the proof method of *double checking the result* known, for example, from solving systems of equations where correctness comparison of inputs and outputs is much easier than to find and generate outputs from given inputs. Formulae representation techniques as in well accepted mathematical proofs are to be utilized, techniques which go beyond predicate logic rule applications.

Our technique exploits the availability of an executable unverified *superHL* compiler. But because of subsequent inspection of special in-output pairs this compiler suffices the demand that it is only used as an intelligent typing assistant. The correctness of the final result

$trans(\pi_{trans}^h)$ does not logically depend on the question whether the *superHL* compiler is generally correct.

The prototype *ComLisp* Compiler employs intermediate languages *SIL* (stack intermediate language), *SubC* (with parameterless procedures and two standard arrays for runtime stack and heap) and *tass (transputer* assembly language). Systematic deliberations prevent from work explosion: E.g. only the final *tass* assembler and a *print* routine need inspections in *transputer* code; inspection for the initial *ComLisp* to *SIL* compiler needs be done in *SIL* only. All languages use the procedure (subroutine) concept, and procedures are translated to procedures. Hence compositional implementation correctness proof documentation is comfortably supported. Instead of in-output comparison by hand it is sometimes rewarding to develop checking programs based on the specifications of passes $trans_i$. Then we have to solve a new implementation correctness problem which is hopefully, but not always less complex than the former. Anyway, for every implementation idea or act applied to π_{trans}^h we can locate document lines which express that the idea or act is correctly performed, an essential characteristic of trustworthy proofs. The work style on translator implementation correctness differs from that on translation specification correctness. The latter is proof work as a mathematician loves it, the former is likewise important, but means more ingeneering-like, mathematically conscientious application of theorems in a large case study.

Reflections on translator implementation correctness should considerably reduce or even cancel necessity of machine code inspections and verifications as they are done still to-day to foster integrity in process control and automatization. As an outgrowth of ProCoS a DFG-project "Verified Translators (Verifix)" with the cooperating Universities of Karlsruhe (G. Goos), Kiel (H. Langmaack) and Ulm (F. W. von Henke) has been set up, a research activity on correctness of translations and compiler implementations as well as on correctness of entire compiler engineering methods and of tools for compiler generation [12].

6.5. Correct Translation of *TimedPL* Programs to *HDL* Hardware Descriptions

TimedPL programs can be directly translated into hardware via provably correct transformations. A *TimedPL* program defines what a hardware circuit should *procedurally* achieve, while an *HDL* description *structurally* expresses the components and their interconnections. J. He, J. Bowen and Z. Jianping [5] present an *HDL* language for *synchronous, globally clocked, discrete time* circuits. An observation-oriented semantics is based on states of the wires of a device. Algebraic laws permit *TimedPL* circuit descriptions to be transformed to *hardware normal form C(s,f).*

C(s,f) is a collection of connected combinational circuits w.**Comb**(W), latches x.**Latch** (B, E), delays e.**Delay**(L), combinational output circuits d.**Out**(D) and input wires c.**In**. w, x, e, d and c act as different names for different hardware components; W, B, E, L and D are Boolean expressions of the names w, x, b and c saying how components are connected by wires to one another and to the environment. Any cycle must be cut by a latch. s is a distinguished input wire through which the environment triggers the circuit. f is a distinguished output wire with f.**Out**($\bar{f}$)&$\bar{f}$.**Delay**(F) signalling the operation finish of network *C(s,f)* after at least one clock cycle. *C(s,f)* must comply with so called *normal form laws*.

As in section 6.4.1 J. He's, J. Bowen's and Z. Jianping's idea is to prove translation theorems from *TimedPL* program constructs to normal form circuits using algebraic refinement laws for *TimedPL* processes. These theorems implicitly yield correct inductive translation specifications. The necessary semantic link is provided by an *interpreter* for normal form circuits $C(s,f)$ written in *TimedPL*. Hardware compilation has been investigated for some time; ProCoS presents systematic techniques how to prove such compilation correct.

Hardware normal form is fairly close to the typical notation in hardware *netlist* languages describing the interconnections of basic digital components. Netlists can be implemented by field programmable gate arrays (*FPGAs*) which are dynamically reconfigurable by software. All what we have said about translator implementation verification in section 6.4.2 remains applicable. As soon as we have a correct translation specification it does not matter for correct translator implementation whether the final binary code is for von Neumann-processors or for *FPGAS*.

6.6. From Discrete-State Dynamical Systems to VLSI Circuits

Most of the ProCoS activities described so far are concerned with formally relating and transforming different discrete-state descriptions of dynamical systems, resulting in time-related automata descriptions of various kinds. As discrete-state descriptions of circuits provide a highly abstracted view of the detailed physical behaviour of circuits, this calls for yet another link between formal semantic theories: Behavioral descriptions of circuits using discrete states have to be linked to more detailed continuous state-models (e.g. SPICE-like models [1]). Note that this issue is not only a completion of the ProCoS-tower, but is indeed crucial to any hybrid systems theory [13] as all these theories start from the postulate that the influence of discrete controllers on the overall system's trajectory is adequately modeled by discontinuities. Note, furthermore, that bridging the semantic gap between discrete and continuous descriptions of circuits cannot currently by accomplished through standard results of circuit theory, but is a field of growing interest to the hardware verification community [15, 28, 24, 46, 14, 3].

Within ProCoS we have been able to establish a firm link between discrete and continuous models of circuits, which provides a basis for asynchronous circuit design from architectural specifications in Duration Calculus (cf. section 6.1) as well as for derivation of additional timing conditions necessary in VLSI implementation of synchronous controllers (section 6.5). Currently, our models [8, 9] cover the dynamics of hybrid systems which have their discrete components built from MOS transistors. Similar models should – except for variations in timing parameters – apply for any other implementation technologies of digital components. In [8], we start from a continuous behavioral model of MOS transistors [42, 30, 43], which we state in a form that uses several under-determined physical parameters in order to achieve physical adequacy, thereby also reducing the problem of parameter extraction. By resorting to a statement about the physical bounds of sensor and actuator performance, e.g. their latencies, we can then derive discrete-state and even discrete-time models of MOS transistor dynamic behavior from the continuous behavioral model. The derived models, which are mainly in terms of *timed leads to* properties determining gate output values whenever gate inputs have been stable for a sufficiently long time period, are such that any conclusion drawn from them when analyzing a hybrid system will be met by the collection of MOS transistors actually implementing the discrete components, when the physical accuracy of the circuit-level behavioral model of MOS transistors is given. So we are provided with models for the development and analysis of hybrid systems.

Derivation of these models has revealed some surprising further insights. Generally, three-valued models are used when meta-stability is possible, as then two-valued models are intuitively unsound. But — just using a model where switching delays are only bounded from above instead of the idealized view that switching delays are deterministic — we have found two- and three-valued models to coincide. Hence, three-valuedness of design models is *not* an immediate consequence of design contexts where meta-stability is unavoidable.

Furthermore, some amount of decidability has been gained at no cost, as a discrete-time model has been shown to coincide with its continuous-time counterpart. This suggests that some of the undecidability results for real-time logics are irrelevant to implementation development, as they rely on existence of small-scale differences between trajectories which are undetectable by physical devices. Hence, it raises the question whether less complex real-time logics can be designed, based on the insight that any reactive systems is band-limited in its reactive behavior.

7. Conclusions

The main achievement of ProCoS is to have related the semantic models of several different system development levels and to have shown up how to mathematically verify the transitions between these levels w.r.t. the semantic relations. In models of lower levels, as well as in transition rules from higher levels towards implementations, physical restrictions of real-time hardware behavior have been taken into consideration instead of creating a theoretical edifice which is as plain as possible, e.g. latency instead of maximum progress.

ProCoS is working on a common universal model to support synthesis and verification of systems. A sequential algebra of sets of observations is one approach [23]. Algebraic laws are used to help in software and hardware compilation [19, 10].

The products of the different development stages for specific simple case studies are comparatively easy to find. The main problem and burden of ProCoS is to get the principal structures of languages, interfaces, correctness notions, proofs and proof methods right. So, for example, consideration of translation correctness is targeting at code for a real processor, the *transputer*, and at an attempt to modularize the whole proof in small steps which are controllable and provable independently.

There are still open problems. Describing system components by logical formulae and composing them by logical conjunction is a modest approach to modularity. Encapsulation capabilities are needed for modularity and scalability. A further problem is the reach of the requirements analysis approach. Realistic physical, chemical, biological processes reveal difficult parameter extractions so that system dynamics can be described only insufficiently. So one might question whether formal development of functional requirements is possible in general or should be confined to safety-critical components. This leads to the problem of integration with other control system concepts: classical, knowledge-based, fuzzy or neural concepts.

Acknowledgments

I would like to thank J.P. Bowen, M. Fränzle, B. von Karger, M. Müller-Olm and A.P. Ravn for stimulating discussions. The research explained in this article is supported by the Commission of the European Union CEU, Brussels, and by the Deutsche Forschungsgemeinschaft DFG, Bonn.

References

1. P. Antognetti and G. Massobrio. *Semiconductor Device Modelling with SPICE*. McGraw-Hill, 1988.
2. F. L. Bauer, H. Ehlers, A. Horsch, B. Möller, H. Partsch, O. Paukner, and P. Pepper. *The Munich Project CIP, vol. II: The Transformation System CIP-S*, volume 292 of *LNCS*. Springer-Verlag, 1987.
3. R. D. Black. Towards a dynamical systems approach to asynchronous circuit design. Internal report, Department of Computer Science, University of Waterloo, Canada, 1994.
4. J. P. Bowen, editor. *Towards Verified Systems*, volume 2 of *Real-Time and Safety-Critical Systems Series*. Elsevier, 1994.
5. J. P. Bowen, C. A. R. Hoare, M. R. Hansen, A. P. Ravn, H. Rischel, E.-R. Olderog, M. Schenke, M. Fränzle, M. Müller-Olm, J. He, and Z. Jianping. Provably correct systems — FTRTFT'94 tutorial. ProCoS Technical Report COORD JB 7/1, Oxford University Computing Laboratory, UK, September 1994.
6. J. P. Bowen et al. A ProCoS II project description: ESPRIT Basic Research Project 7071. *Bull. EATCS*, 50:128–137, 1993.
7. K.-H. Buth. Automated code generator verification based on algebraic laws. ProCoS Technical Report Kiel KHB 5/1, Christian-Albrechts-Universität Kiel, Germany, September 1995.
8. M. Fränzle. A discrete model of VLSI dynamics in hybrid control applications. ProCoS Technical Report Kiel MF 17/3, Christian-Albrechts-Universität Kiel, Germany, April 1995.
9. M. Fränzle. From continuity to discreteness — five views of embedded control hardware. ProCoS Technical Report Kiel MF 18/1, Christian-Albrechts-Universität Kiel, Germany, August 1995.
10. M. Fränzle and M. Müller-Olm. Towards provably correct code generation for a hard real-time programming language. In Peter A. Fritzson, editor, *Compiler Construction*, volume 786 of *LNCS*, pages 294–308. Springer-Verlag, 1994.
11. M.-C. Gaudel. Advantages and limits of formal approaches for ultra-high dependability. In Randell et al. [37], pages 241–252.
12. G. Goos, H. Langmaack, F. W. von Henke, W. Goerigk, and W. Zimmermann. Verifizierte Übersetzer (Verifix). DFG-Projektantrag, Karlsruhe, Kiel, Ulm, 1994.
13. R. L. Grossman, A. Nerode, A. P. Ravn, and H. Rischel, editors. *Hybrid Systems*, volume 736 of *LNCS*. Springer-Verlag, 1993.
14. F. K. Hanna. Reasoning about real circuits. In T. F. Melham and J. Camilleri, editors, *Higher Order Logic Theorem Proving and its Applications*, volume 859 of *LNCS*. Springer-Verlag, September 1994.
15. F. K. Hanna and N. Daeche. Specification and verification using higher-order logic: A case study. In George Milne and P. A. Subrahmanyam, editors, *Formal Aspects of VLSI Design*. North-Holland, 1985.
16. J. He, C. A. R. Hoare, M. Fränzle, M. Müller-Olm, E.-R. Olderog, M. Schenke, M. R. Hansen, A. P. Ravn, and H. Rischel. Provably correct systems. In Langmaack et al. [26], pages 288–335.
17. J. He and J. Zheng. Simulation approach to provably correct hardware compilation. In Langmaack et al. [26], pages 336–350.
18. C. A. R. Hoare. *Communicating Sequential Processes*. Series in Computer Science. Prentice Hall, 1985.
19. C. A. R. Hoare, J. He, and A. Sampaio. Normal form approach to compiler design. *Acta Inform.*, 30:701–739, 1994.
20. W. A. Hunt jr. FM 8501: A verified microprocessor. Technical Report 47, Univ. of Texas, Austin, 1986.
21. Inmos ltd. *occam 2 Reference Manual*. Series in Computer Science. Prentice-Hall International, 1988.
22. Inmos ltd. *Transputer Instruction Set: A compiler writer's guide*. Prentice-Hall International, 1988.
23. B. von Karger and C. A. R. Hoare. Sequential calculus. *Information Processing Letters*, 53(3):123–130, 1995.

24. R. P. Kurshan and K. L. McMillan. Analysis of digital circuits through symbolic reduction. *IEEE Transact. Comp. Aid. Des.*, 10(11):1356–1371, November 1991.

25. H. Langmaack and A. P. Ravn. The ProCoS project: Provably correct systems. In Bowen [4], pages 249–265.

26. H. Langmaack, W.-P. de Roever, and J. Vytopil, editors. *Formal Techniques in Real-Time and Fault-Tolerant Systems*, volume 863 of *LNCS*. Springer-Verlag, September 1994.

27. B. Littlewood and L. Strigini. Validation of ultra-high dependability for software-based systems. In Randell et al. [37], pages 473–494.

28. A. J. Martin. Programming in VLSI. In C. A. R. Hoare, editor, *Developments in Concurrency and Communication*, The University of Texas at Austin Year of Programming Series, chapter 1. Addison-Wesley, 1990.

29. J S. Moore. Piton: A verified assembly level language. Technical Report 22, Computational Logic Inc., Austin, Texas, 1988.

30. A. Möschwitzer and K. Lunze. *Halbleiterelektronik*. VEB Verlag Technik, eighth edition, 1988.

31. M. Müller-Olm. A new proposal for TimedPL's semantics. ProCoS Technical Report Kiel MMO 10/2, Christian-Albrechts-Universität Kiel, Germany, August 1994.

32. M. Müller-Olm. Compiling the gas burner case study. ProCoS Technical Report Kiel MMO 16/1, Christian-Albrechts-Universität Kiel, Germany, August 1995.

33. M. Müller-Olm. Structuring code generator correctness proofs by stepwise abstracting the machine language's semantics. ProCoS Technical Report Kiel MMO 12/3, Christian-Albrechts-Universität Kiel, Germany, January 1995.

34. M. Müller-Olm. *Modular Compiler Verification*. Dissertation, Univ. Kiel, 1996. To be published as Vol. 1283 of LNCS, Springer-Verlag, 1997.

35. E.-R. Olderog. *Nets, Terms and Formulas*. Cambridge Tracts in Theoretical Computer Science. Cambridge University Press, 1991.

36. E.-R. Olderog and C. A. R. Hoare. Specification-oriented semantics for communicating processes. *Acta Informatica*, 23:9–66, 1986.

37. B. Randell, J.-C. Laprie, H. Kopetz, and B. Littlewood, editors. *Predictably Dependable Computing Systems*, ESPRIT Basic Research Series. Springer-Verlag, 1995.

38. A. P. Ravn. Design of embedded real-time computing systems. Lecture Notes, Danish Technical University, Lyngby, Denmark, September 1994.

39. W. Reisig. *Petri Nets, An Introduction*. EATCS Monographs on Theoretical Computer Science. Springer-Verlag, 1985.

40. M. Schenke. Specification and transformation of reactive systems with time restrictions and concurrency. In Langmaack et al. [26], pages 605–620.

41. M. Schenke and E.-R. Olderog. Design of real-time systems: From duration calculus to correct programs. ProCoS Technical Report OLD MS 17/1, Univ. Oldenburg, Germany, August 1995.

42. H. Shichman and D. A. Hodges. Modeling and simulation of insulated-gate field-effect transistor switching circuits. *IEEE J. SSC.*, pages 285–289, 1968.

43. J. Singh. *Semiconductor Devices*. McGraw-Hill Series in Electrical and Computer Engineering. McGraw-Hill, 1994.

44. J. U. Skakkebæk. *A Verification Assistant for a Real-Time Logic*. PhD thesis, Dep. Comp. Sc. TUD Lyngby, 1994.

45. J. M. Spivey. *The Z Notation. A Reference Manual*. International Series in Computer Science. Prentice-Hall, second edition, 1992.

46. P. R. Stephan and R. K. Brayton. Physically realizable gate models. Technical Report UCB/ERL M93/33, Electronics Research Laboratory, University of California, Berkeley, May 1993.

47. W. D. Young. A verified code generator for a subset of Gypsy. Technical Report 33, Computational Logic Inc., Austin, Texas, 1988.

48. W. D. Young. System verification and the CLI stack. In Bowen [4], pages 225–248.

49. C. Zhou, C. A. R. Hoare, and A. P. Ravn. A calculus of durations. *Inform. Proc. Letters*, 40(5):269–276, 1991.

50. C. Zhou, A. P. Ravn, and M. R. Hansen. An extended duration calculus for hybrid real-time systems. In Grossman et al. [13], pages 36–59.

Real-Time Systems, 13, 277–302 (1997)

Building Large, Complex, Distributed Safety-Critical Operating Systems

HORST F. WEDDE   wedde@ls3.informatik.uni-dortmund.de

JON A. LIND   lind@ls3.informatik.uni-dortmund.de

Informatik III, University of Dortmund, 44221 Dortmund Germany

Abstract. Safety-critical systems typically operate in unpredictable environments. Requirements for safety and reliability are in conflict with those for real-time responsiveness. Due to unpredictable environmental needs there is no static trade-off between measures to accommodate the conflicting objectives. Instead every feature or operating system service has to be *adaptive*. Finally, for any design problem, there cannot be any closed-form (formal) approach taking care at the same time of (external) time constraints or deadlines, and synchronization requirements in distributed design. The reason is that these two aspects are *causally independent*. - In this situation we worked out a heuristic experimental, performance-driven and performance-based methodology that allows in an educated way to start with a coarse system model, with accurate logical expectations regarding its behavior. Through experiments these expectations are validated. If they are found to successfully stand the tests extended expectations and model features are generated for refining the previous design as well as its performance criteria. The refinement is done in such a way that the previous experimental configurations are extreme model cases or data profiles which both logically and experimentally are to reproduce the behavior of the previous modeling step. Thus the novel performance aspects or tendencies could then unambiguously be attributed to the influences of the refined model features. We termed this methodology *Incremental Experimentation*. As a *general* methodology it relies on a *principle of comparative performance studies* rather than on realistic data for narrow application ranges.

The paper describes how we applied a 5-step design and refinement procedure for developing, analyzing, and evaluating our distributed operating system MELODY that exhibits novel services for supporting real-time and safety-critical applications in unpredictable environments. Experimental set-ups and theme-related findings are discussed in particular.

Keywords: distributed real-time systems, distributed operating systems, distributed file systems, safety-critical systems, performance-driven design, comparative performance, distributed task and resource scheduling

1. Introduction

Safety-Critical systems. In *safety-critical systems* (such as nuclear power plants, automated robot control systems, automatic landing systems for aircraft, etc.) tasks not only have to meet deadlines, but most of these are critical in the sense that the system would not survive in case of a certain number of deadline failures of subsequent task instances. In such a critical stage, a task instance is said to have become **essentially critical**. However, beyond this special real-time responsiveness (here the successful handling of essentially critical task instances that we have termed **survivability** (Wedde et al., 1991)), safety-critical systems must also satisfy rigid **dependability** requirements (reliability and fault tolerance). In order to meet as many of these **conflicting requirements**, in environments that are typically unpredictable, a very high amount of **adaptability** of system functions is demanded. Safety-critical systems have gained rapidly increasing relevance in research and development, both industrial and commercial, and are **typically distributed**. All this makes

61

even the design of large safety-critical systems an extraordinarily complex modeling and engineering challenge.

Incremental Experimentation. Synchronization in distributed systems and timing constraints (regarding external or environmental time) are causally independent. Consequently there are no closed-form design approaches for distributed safety-critical systems but **only heuristic modeling and analysis procedures**. Due to the large number of relevant parameters, and to their unclear interdependence, a heuristic design methodology cannot at the same time be realistic and transparent to the designer. As the basis of this paper we will discuss significant issues of a novel approach to the design of distributed safety-critical systems, termed **Incremental Experimentation**. This is a heuristic experimental, performance-driven and performance-based methodology that allows in an educated way to start with a coarse system model, with accurate logical expectations regarding its behavior. Through experiments, these expectations are validated. If they are found to successfully stand the tests extended expectations and model features are generated for refining the previous design as well as its performance criteria. The refinement is also done in such a way that the previous experimental configurations are extreme model cases or data profiles which both logically and experimentally are to reproduce the behavior of the previous modeling step. Thus the novel performance aspects, or tendencies, could unambiguously be attributed to the influences of the refined model features.

MELODY. In the MELODY project a distributed real-time operating system has been developed that is tailored to the requirements of safety-critical systems. It was started at Wayne State University in Detroit, Michigan, and is now in the phase of an operational distributed lab prototype in our labs at the University of Dortmund, Germany. Previous stages of the MELODY project have been reported in (Wedde et al., 1990, Wedde and Xu, 1992, Wedde et al., 1993, Wedde et al., 1994). Although valuable work has been reported on studying in detail hardware or software monitoring concepts (Haben and Shin, 1990, Jahanian et al., 1994) as well as the potential advantages of off-line task scheduling for hard real-time systems (Xu and Parnas, 1993) such discussions have never been integrated into a comprehensive view including e.g. resource scheduling issues. Likewise these approaches do not take into account the unpredictability in safety-critical environments thus adaptivity has not been addressed. While we are eager to include all techniques and considerations for improving details of single operating system service functions at later stages of implementation and distributed experiments, we considered it particularly important for MELODY to integrate *all* relevant design and analysis aspects into a realistic and pragmatic modeling methodology in a systematic way, at the same time reconciling the conflicting issues.

Organization of the Paper. In the following section the Incremental Experimentation methodology is described as we used it in the MELODY system design. While technical performance details and service functions had been thoroughly discussed in the operating system context and under application service needs (Wedde et al., 1990, Wedde and Xu, 1992, Wedde et al., 1993, Wedde et al., 1994) the emphasis here is rather on the methodological aspects of our work. Thus performance discussions are reported only in order to support the details of model development and refinement steps. Conclusions and future directions comprise the last section.

2. The MELODY Project : A Study for Incremental Experimentation

In the development of the MELODY system through using Incremental Experimentation progress was made from phase to phase by using expectations based on performance results from the prior phase. Refinements to MELODY could then be validated by selecting extreme ranges for the new parameters (either for the choice of model or task/data profiles) that covered the previous model. Under these conditions the results from the prior phase would have to be matched. Only then could we fully understand and analyze the result of the current phase, in particular attribute tendencies safely to the refined parameters. MELODY has currently progressed through five phases of Incremental Experimentation. Below we outline the progression through these five phases, resulting in the development of a satisfactory reactive system prototype. Phases beyond are under investigation right now. Due to page limitations we will frequently refer to previous publications for technical details.

2.1. Phase 1 : The MELODY File System

The first step in the MELODY project was to design novel file system functions tailored to safety-critical requirements. They are both sensitive to real-time constraints and adaptable to the needs in the unpredictable environments in which safety-critical systems typically operate. MELODY maintains two types of file copies: **Public Copies** which are kept mutually consistent, and **Private Copies** which are only refreshed after a public copy update. *Write tasks always work on the public copies of a file. For this first file system model it was throughout assumed that* **read** *tasks could be accommodated either by public file copies or by private copies, the latter ones being locally available.* For each public copy there exists a **Shadow copy** from which tasks would read even while the corresponding public copy is updated, thus providing for concurrent read/write access to files. (This technique has been used frequently for non-replicated files, and has been extensively described in the literature.) For meeting the real-time constraints the number and location of public and private file copies are closely monitored by a novel **File Assigner** service described below, in order to minimize remote access as well as the overhead for consistency maintenance.

Tasks represent control functions, corrective actions etc. They are executed on a regular basis. Every occurrence of a task is termed a **task instance** or **incarnation**. In MELODY, due to the unpredictability of the environment typical in many safety-critical applications, they are assumed to be aperiodic in nature. Also they may be executing on dedicated processors. File access is done using remote file operations rather than task migration or file transfer to the accessing site. Each task is a small-scale, transaction-like operation with just one segment of task activity termed **critical section** in which it accesses a number of objects (copies of possibly different files) concurrently. Write operations work on **all** *public* copies of a file, through remote local write operations. Read operations read from *one* copy (public or private). We also assumed that task execution times on each local file copy could be determined within tight bounds.

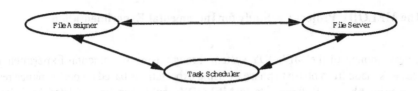

Figure 1. MELODY Management Functions at Each Node

Three major system modules interact at each node: **File Server, File Assigner, Task Scheduler** (fig. 1). Each module is briefly described below, a detailed specification can be found in (Wedde et al., 1990).

File Server (FS): Each FS engages in concurrently allocating the needed files for k tasks in its queue according to algorithms tailored to the application area involved. Upon learning of an update to a public copy, FS, at a site holding a private copy, will request to refresh the private copy using a remote procedure call from a site holding a public copy. FS also maintains a read/write access history for each file requested by a task. This is used to calculate **an estimated execution time** (EET_j) for a task instance T_j *with the list of files needed by T_j in its critical section* (LRF_j):

$$EET_j = \texttt{Estimated\_Computation\_Time}(T_j) + \sum_{r \in LRF_j} \texttt{Computation\_Time}(r)$$

where $\texttt{Estimated\_Computation\_Time}$ for T_j is determined as the average of the corresponding values of the last 5 instances of T_j, and $\texttt{Computation\_Time}$ is the time to access the needed copies of file r, including the communication time for the possibly involved remote operations.

Task Scheduler (TS): TS schedules a set of k tasks that have arrived at a site I according to a scheduling policy tailored to the applicational needs. A task T_j arriving at site I (unpredictably), would be considered for scheduling using the following parameters:

EET_j :   Estimated Execution Time of a task T_j;
DT_j :   Deadline for task T_j;
LRF_j :   List of required files,
            containing for every file its identifier and access pattern;
PrT_j :   Static priority.

Upon arrival of T_j, the local TS communicates with the local FS to check which of the files in LRF_j is locally available, and calculates an estimate for the actual execution time based on EET_j. Tasks are then placed into the local task queue (**LTQ**) according to their order of execution, and dispatched for execution from this queue. *As a result of the unpredictability of the environment, and the ensuing typical aperiodicity of task instance occurrences, task scheduling in MELODY is non-preemptive.*

TS also characterizes tasks as either: *Strongly Schedulable* (T_j can be inserted into LTQ and meet its deadline), *Weakly Schedulable* (T_j is decided to fail but could have met its deadline in case that all files from LRF_j had been locally available), or non-schedulable.

A deadline failure count for every file that is used by a task is incremented upon every deadline failure. If this count exceeds a preset threshold value, the local TS issues a request to the local FA to obtain a copy of the file.

File Assigners (FA): In our model a trade-off has to be made, under changing request and deadline failure patterns, between the costs of serving file requests with a given distribution of public and private copies, and the costs for realizing various alternative distributions. The term "costs" here denotes time delays for overhead operations, communication and transmission delays, both for remote and internal communication. The alternatives for public and private copies are:

- relocating a public copy to the requesting site;

- making an additional public copy available to the site of the requesting task;

- deleting a file copy if there were not enough requests over a period of time;

- establishing a private copy at a site.

The FA cooperates with the FS and TS and remote FAs in order to manage replication, relocation, and deletion of files within the MELODY file system. Particularly the deletion of a public copy requires the agreement of all FAs holding a copy of the file, assuring a minimum number of copies of a file that may be required to be maintained for reliability purposes. A public copy will be granted upon a FS request by a local TS, if and only if no potentially granting site would suffer, either the through the lack of a relocated copy or the additional overhead for an additional public copy, in such a way that - based on the local task execution history - FA would have to request a copy back in turn. First a public copy relocation would be requested. If denied, a replication is sought. If not possible, a private copy will be granted.

In this initial phase (Wedde et al., 1990) MELODY's file system was compared to less flexible models exhibiting only some of MELODY's functionality yet lower overhead: **Base**, **Public** and **Private Copy** models. In the **Base** model the FAs are deactivated, and the FSs do not provide for replication and relocation. The **Public Copy** model provides public copies of files that could be relocated or replicated, but allows for no private copies. The **Private Copy** model allows for one public copy which could be relocated but not replicated, and multiple private copies, resulting in a weak concurrency protocol requiring less communication overhead (no distributed updates or consensus protocols). In the other direction, we wanted to compare the potential benefit of MELODY's adaptive features with a logically ideal yet unrealistic model. Here a central FA is assumed to always have the latest information about the optimal file copy distribution, so it would not to spend any communication time on this issue. This was modeled in our experiments by replacing the MELODY FA functions by a central FA for which the communication overhead was counted as zero. The resulting experimental model was termed **Ideal Case** model.

In the task profiles the distribution of read and write access requests differed widely in order to scale and normalize the experimental findings in the following sense. It seemed reasonable that the Private Copy model would do better than the Public Copy model once there was a high dominance of read requests. The reason is that the comparably few updates could easily be accommodated by refreshing private copies at the requesting sites, whereas in the Public Copy model a large amount of overhead would be encountered even for satisfying read requests by providing a multitude of public copies. Conversely, it was expected that the Public Copy model would perform better than the Private Copy model in case of a high dominance of write requests from tasks. Private copies would have to be refreshed with a high frequency, and each time a complete file would be transmitted to the sites holding a private copy, while the write operations would typically only work on a moderate number of records. Based on these heuristics we generated task profiles with an amount of 20 − 30% of read operations and 70 − 80% of write operations. Correspondingly another profile was generated with 20 − 30% of write operations and 70 − 80% of read operations. A third profile was also generated that uniformly distributed the number of read and write operations. A more extensive experimental set-up is to be found in (Wedde et al., 1990). Since, for example, the write dominance profile was designed to favor the Public Copy model this should show up in the curves. If so, the other comparisons could be more securely interpreted based on the shape and relative positions of the curves describing the performance of the Public and Private Copy models. At this point it was merely a conjecture that MELODY would do better than the Public Copy model.

The results under the write dominance profile (fig. 2), show very clearly that the performance of the Public Copy model is throughout better than the Private Copy model. The results for the read dominance profile (fig. 3) show that the Private Copy model does better than the Public Copy model. In all cases, MELODY's additional adaptive features make its performance better than either the Public or Private Copy models. The uniform distribution profile (fig. 4), shows that the Public and Private Copy model have no clear advantage

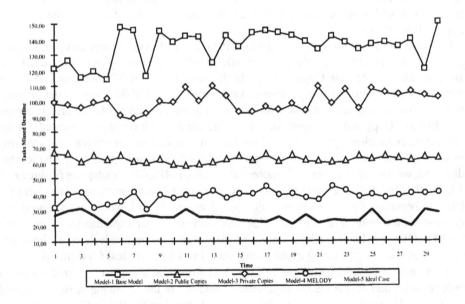

Figure 2. Write Dominance

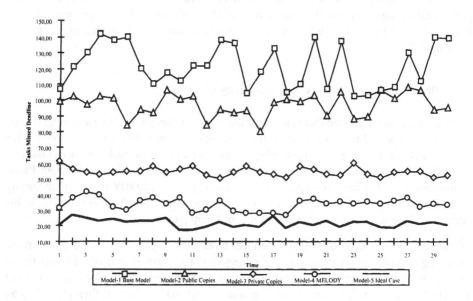

Figure 3. Read Dominance

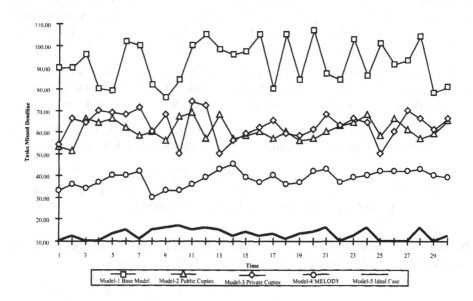

Figure 4. Uniform Read / Write

over each other, while MELODY still clearly outperforms both. Also, while MELODY performed throughout worse than the fictive Ideal Case model, it exhibits the same adaptive tendencies as the latter one, behaving as a kind of real world implementation of the Ideal Case model.

2.2. Phase 2 & 3 : Criticality and Sensitivity of Tasks

In Phase 1 we had neglected that tasks and their instances have in practice a varying degree to which they would be sensitive to latest information (from public copies) - *this applies to read tasks only* -, or how long deadline failures of subsequent task instances could be tolerated without endangering the whole system's survivability. The results from Phase 1 provides us with a basis of expectation, for refining the MELODY model by including criticality and sensitivity measures. (This will be apparent through the discussion in this section.) These will be determined through 2 different parameters:

Definition. (1) For each site I site-dependent thresholds a_i' and a_i'' (which could be read-justed e.g. under changing hardware technology) will represent a *frame of criticality* for all tasks arriving at I. Each task T_j at site I is in turn assigned an individual *criticality value* C_j. If $C_j \geq a_i''$ then T_j is considered as a *non-critical* task, if $C_j \leq a_i'$ then the task is an *essentially critical* task. If $a_i' < C_j < a_i''$ the task is called *critical*.

Similarly:

Definition. (2) For each site I site-dependent thresholds b_i' and b_i'' will represent a *frame of sensitivity* for all tasks arriving at I. Each task T_j at site I is in turn assigned an individual *sensitivity value* R_j. If $R_j \geq b_i''$ then task T_j is called as *robust*. If $R_j \leq b_i'$ the task is considered as *essentially sensitive*. If $b_i' < R_j < b_i''$ the task is called *sensitive*.

C_j and R_j are understood as criticality and sensitivity values of the initial instance of task T_j which might have been experimentally determined, tailored to the application. Then, the **essential step** is to define **relative degrees of criticality and sensitivity**, respectively:

Definition. (3) Let C_j be the criticality value of T_j, and T_{jk} the k-th instance or incarnation of T_j. The *relative criticality of instance* T_{jk} is an integer which is defined as follows:

$$C_{jk} := \begin{cases} C_j; & C_j \leq a_i' \text{ or } C_j \geq a_i'' \text{ or} \\ & T_{j(k-1)} \text{ met its deadline} \\ \max\{(C_j - \texttt{Failures}(T_j)), a_i'\}; & \text{otherwise} \end{cases}$$

Definition. (4) Let R_j be the sensitivity value of T_j, and T_{jk} the k-th instance of T_j. The *relative sensitivity of instance* T_{jk} is an integer R_{jk} defined as follows:

$$R_{jk} := \begin{cases} R_j; & R_j \leq b_i' \text{ or } R_j \geq b_i'' \text{ or} \\ & T_{j(k-1)} \text{ met its deadline} \\ \min\{(R_j + \texttt{Failures}(T_j)), b_i''\}; & \text{otherwise} \end{cases}$$

Note. Failures(T_j) is the number of instance failures after the last successful instance completion.

Thus the relative criticality (relative sensitivity) of the instances of T_j is constant if T_j is essentially critical or non-critical (essentially sensitive or robust). Also, once the threshold values a_i' or b_i'' have been reached by a task instance T_{jk} the value C_{jk} does not change, except after successful completion of T_{jk}. Finally the instance T_{jk} of task T_j is called *critical, non-critical, or essentially critical (sensitive, robust, or essentially sensitive)* depending how C_{jk} (R_{jk}) relates to the threshold values a_i', a_i'' (b_i', b_i'') as given in def.1 and def.2 .

Criticality and sensitivity of a task are heuristically determined through the application system or the system environment (as are deadlines). In an automated landing system certain corrective actions - like trajectory adjustments before touching ground - have to be completed under increasingly rigid time limits

- in order to allow, under unpredictably changing wind conditions (e.g. gusty wind), for subsequent adjustments that would altogether guarantee the correct angle with respect to the runway;

- since the delay of the aircraft's reaction (ca. 4 seconds for a Boeing 747) makes a correction after a certain point of time obsolete. If the course is still wrong at this time the aircraft may crash onto the runway.

If visual information was to be used - like for independent robots in Outer Space - then the deadlines of some task instances could possibly be missed, depending on the amount of "unexpected" information in the frames under processing. The closer a critical point of time comes after which a collision with another object becomes unavoidable, the more urgently have the deadlines of corrective tasks to be met. In the sense of def.1 and def.3 these tasks and their instances becomes more and more critical. The last instance of a task with a deadline before the "point of no return" must not fail since otherwise the robot (and thus the computer system inside) are endangered to be destroyed.

Tasks such as described in the last paragraph typically need up-to-date information since the environment as depicted in the visual frames may change quickly and broadly. They are sensitive according to def.2. If it would become too late for the next (essentially) critical instance to complete within its deadline while waiting for the analysis of the latest frames being reflected in the *public file copies*, it is reasonable for the survival of the system to make use instead of local private copies, even care for having such copies available when they are needed. In this way there would be a *chance* to avoid the loss of the system. Correspondingly, with subsequent task instances failing in a row the next instance is considered less sensitive, or more robust. (How this policy is established will be described in the subsequent paragraphs).- In tables 1 and 2 a few task histories should further clarify the concepts.

In table 1, Task T_1 has $C_1 = R_1 = 4$ as initial criticality and sensitivity values, respectively. Instance T_{11} fails to meet its deadline. T_{11}'s failure results in instance T_{12} having a decreased relative criticality $C_{12} = 3$ (i.e. T_{12} is more critical than T_{11}), and an incremented relative sensitivity $R_{12} = 5$ (i.e. T_{12} is more robust than T_{11}). The failure of

Table 1. Sample Failure History for Task T_1 $a_i' := 2 =: b_i'$ $a_i'' := 8 =: b_i''$

Instance #k	1	2	3	4
Status	Failed	Failed	Success	
Criticality C_{1k}	4	3	2	4
Sensitivity R_{1k}	4	5	6	4

instance T_{12} again implies changes of T_{13}'s relative criticality and sensitivity values into 2 and 6, respectively. T_{13} has become essentially critical but completes by its deadline. The success of T_{13} causes T_{14}'s relative criticality and sensitivity values to be reset to the initial values of C_1 and R_1, respectively. However, had instance T_{13} not completed successfully the entire system might no longer have survived since the deadline was essentially critical.

Table 2. Sample Failure History for Task T_2 $a_i' := 2 =: b_i'$ $a_i'' := 8 =: b_i''$

Instance #k	1	2	3	4
Status	Failed	Failed	Success	
Criticality C_{2k}	6	5	4	6
Sensitivity R_{2k}	7	8	8	7

Table 2 shows a failure history for Task T_2 with an initial criticality $C_2 = 6$ and sensitivity $R_2 = 7$. After the failure of T_{21}, instance T_{22} is robust. As also T_{22} fails the relative sensitivity of T_{23} remains at 8 since T_{22} was already robust. Instance T_{23} is able to complete successfully, so T_{24}'s relative criticality and sensitivity values will be set to the initial values C_2 and R_2, respectively.

In order to correctly handle the additional aspects of criticality and sensitivity TS had to be modified. This was done by splitting the *List of Weakly Schedulable Tasks* of the earlier MELODY model into two lists: the *List of Weakly Schedulable Robust Tasks* T_j (i.e. $R_j \geq b_i''$) and the *List of Weakly Schedulable Sensitive Tasks* T_j (i.e. $R_j < b_i''$). Each of the two lists has a threshold (compare 2.1). (Note that during the scheduling phase, TS schedules tasks with $b_i' < R_j' < b_i''$ as sensitive tasks (i.e. they would be found to read public information)).

TS would now schedule task instances according to the following steps :

1. Try to schedule all essentially critical task instances T_{jk} (i.e. $C_{jk}' \leq a_i'$);

2. Schedule critical task instances T_{jk} (i.e. $a_i' < C_{jk}' < a_i''$);

3. Schedule non-critical task instances.

TS invokes FA once one of the thresholds of the Weakly Schedulable Task Lists has been exceeded. FA will request a private copy on behalf of those tasks which are from the Weakly Schedulable Robust Task List, otherwise a public copy for the weakly schedulable tasks that are not essentially critical. If the request is denied then a private copy would be requested only for tasks that are not essentially sensitive. Otherwise the request stops. Additionally, when the next instance of a task would be essentially critical, FA will broadcast a request to have private copies of all needed remote files locally available for this instance. This would ensure local access to the required files that are hoped to be up-to-date to a sufficient extent, thus giving essentially critical tasks a better chance of completing in a timely manner while hoping (in case of a corrective action) that the result would be accurate enough.

Expectation: *Under the extreme case of non-critical and robust tasks the earlier model capabilities are to be logically reflected in the extended model. Hence, for those extreme task profiles the performance should be the same in either model.* Only after this would have been experimentally found, it would be possible to safely attribute experimental tendencies in the refined model under different task settings, to the influence of criticality and/or sensitivity, and separate them from the impact of the earlier MELODY features.

Experimental Set-Up: In the experiments discussed here, 10 *sites* were simulated with 400 *tasks* randomly distributed among all sites. 40 *data files* were randomly distributed among the nodes, each file initially with one public copy and no private copies. In the *task profiles* the parameter ranges - from which random selections were made - were as follows:

The **time units** between task arrival and completion of its scheduling: 10-15

Estimated time for file allocation / task :   10-15

Worst-case task execution time :   3-5

Time after deadline, before next task instance :   0-20

Task Laxity :   10-15

Task Laxity is the amount of time left after successful completion of a task, before the deadline (designed according to the task life model in figure 13). All tasks required the use of 4 – 8 files. The lower and upper threshold values both for criticality and sensitivity were uniformly set to 2 and 8, respectively, across all sites. The task criticality and sensitivity values were varied between 1 and 10. Message delays were counted to range between 3 and 5 units of time. The invocation of TS was assumed to take two units of time, including execution and context switching time. The experimental parameters chosen showed the tendencies of relations between models clearly. The uniformity over all experimental set-ups was chosen because of representational simplicity not because different parameter ranges exhibited different tendencies.

The **performance measurements** were based on the percentage of task failures during a time interval, and equally on **survivability**. *Each simulation was run 10 times with results averaged.* In addition to this we measured survivability in the following way: If an essentially critical task failed during one of the simulation runs then all other runs were counted as failed at the same failure time at which the one run had experienced the failure.

The expected relative performance for the Public Copy and Private Copy models - that were found to be so strongly impacted in the first MELODY model by the dominance of read and write tasks (compare fig.2 and 3) was in fact found to be matched in the refined model, under the assumption of robust tasks only, as indicated in figures 6 and 7.

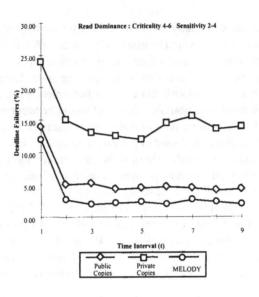

Figure 5. Read Dominance I

For task profiles with small sensitivity values (even close to the threshold to essentially sensitive status, the Public Copy model performed better then the Private Copy model), even under a high dominance of read operations (fig. 5). Based on the findings just discussed (fig.6 and fig.7) it becomes apparent how strong the influence of task sensitivity is. It makes the roles of the Public Copy model and the Private model flip (compare fig.5 and fig.6). In turn, for ranges of increasing values of sensitivity (toward robustness) the Private Copy model eventually performed better than the Public Copy model, which can be attributed, as for the earlier MELODY model, to the low overhead of the Private Copy model for managing private file copies. The situation changes significantly as the number of write operations increases: The Private copy model no longer outperforms the Public Copy model under increasing levels of robustness. Also under a high dominance of write operations both models fail completely (survivability) even for ranges of moderate criticality (fig. 8). Throughout all the simulations runs, MELODY's performance was distinctively superior over the simpler models. It failed only when there was a high dominance of write operations and a very low criticality level. We concluded that for safety-critical systems requiring adaptive measures to operate in unpredictable environments, MELODY's flexibility pays off even under the comparably high overhead, even more so since task sensitivity and criticality have a strong and deteriorating influence on the simpler Public Copy and Private Copy models. More technical details can be found in (Wedde et al., 1993).

2.3. Phase 4 : Distributed Real-Time Resource Scheduling Algorithms

At the same time as phases 2 and 3 were being completed, novel *distributed resource scheduling algorithms* had been defined and validated in extensive comparative simulation

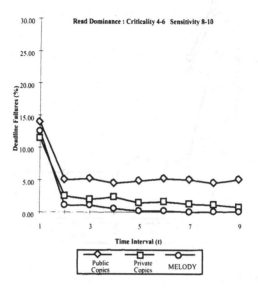

Figure 6. Read Dominance II

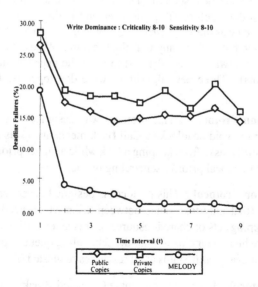

Figure 7. Write Dominance I

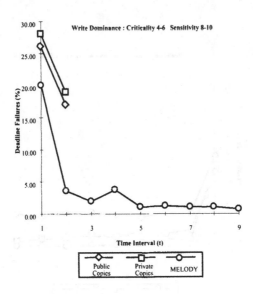

Figure 8. Write Dominance II

experiments (Daniels, 1992, Wedde et al., 1991, Wedde, 1994). In the previous modeling phases resource scheduling (i.e. distributed file copy allocation) had been simulated through simple measures and under uniformity assumptions on the time required by a task to acquire resources and to enter its critical section. This was done since on this topic no appropriate research had been done before. In prior research the distributed resource scheduling algorithm mostly quoted was the *Total Ordering* protocol (Havender, 1968), both deadlock-free and starvation-free but without any real-time feature. We used it as a benchmark for evaluating our protocols (which were the first to meet the needs coming from distributed real-time requirements). Three new algorithms were developed by Douglas C. Daniels (Daniels, 1992):

- **Priority Insertion Protocol** : This protocol was designed to minimize priority inversion. In order to avoid deadlocks a Call Back mechanism was included that would prevent lower priority tasks from keeping a lock while a higher priority task was already scheduled ahead in a local priority scheduling queue.

- **Delayed Insertion Protocol** : This protocol is designed to reduce the effects of Cascaded Blocking (that may take place between tasks which need mutually exclusive access to overlapping sets of shared resources). It is an extension of the Priority Insertion Protocol in which the inclusion into the scheduling queue is preceded by the tasks T_j needing to achieve a *ready* status at all resources requested (file copies from LRF_j).

- **On-the-Fly Protocol** : In order to eliminate Cascaded Blocking completely this protocol employs an *abort (suspend) and restart* strategy. A priority schedule is used to determine the winning task at a resource that has received a lock grant at all resources (file copies from LRF_j), while all other tasks are determined to be losers. Losers will be suspended and placed into a local *sleep list* while being forgotten by all other resource managers. When a busy resource is released, the scheduler will look at its sleep list for candidates to be awakened and restarted.

More technical details are available through (Wedde, 1994). Extensive simulation was done in order to evaluate the comparative performance of the novel protocols. Task scheduling itself was assumed to be only elementary. Simulation criteria were again the total deadline failure rates (figures 9-11) and survivability (fig.12). Experiments examined the performance of the protocols considering deadline margins (fig. 9), task execution times (fig. 10), and task arrival rates (fig. 11).

Experimental Set-Up: The experiments each involved 40 *tasks* competing for 20 *resources*. All tasks required the use of 2-5 resources. The message delay was set to one unit of simulation time. Each simulation was run for 30,000 units of simulation time. In the *task profiles* relevant parameter ranges are as follows for the specified sets of experiments :

Influence of Deadline Margins on Deadline Failure Rates :

Estimated time for file allocation / task :	20 - 40
Worst-case task execution time :	5 - 10
Task Laxity before Deadline :	see chart
Time after deadline, before next task instance occurrence:	20-40

Influence of Execution Times on Deadline Failure Rates :

Estimated time for file allocation / task :	20 - 40
Worst-case task execution time :	see chart
Task Laxity before Deadline :	0 - 40
Time after deadline, before next task instance occurrence:	20 - 40

Influence of Arrival Rates on Deadline Failure Rates :

Estimated time for file allocation / task :	20 - 40
Worst-case task execution time :	5 - 40
Task Laxity before Deadline :	10
Time after deadline, before next task instance occurrence:	see chart

Survivability Analysis :

Estimated time for file allocation / task :	20 - 40
Worst-case task execution time :	5 - 40
Task Laxity before Deadline :	10
Time after deadline, before next task instance occurrence:	20 - 40

For the first three experiments the tasks were assumed to be non-critical. In the **survivability** experiments, 50 different task profiles were randomly chosen from the parameter ranges given above. They were randomly ordered, and for every profile the simulation experiments were executing as long as no essentially critical deadline was missed, up to 30000 time units. (In the latter alternative it was assumed that there would not be a catastrophic failure in the future). Figure 12 depicts, for each of the 50 task profiles, the earliest time among the 10 simulation runs at which an essentially critical deadline was missed.- The initial criticality of tasks was chosen between 0 to 23, were 0 was defined to be essentially critical.

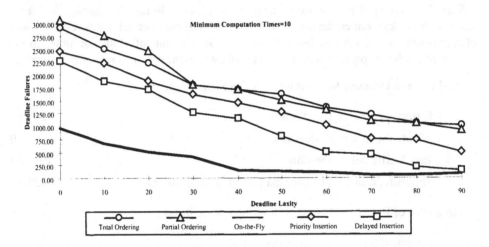

Figure 9. Laxity

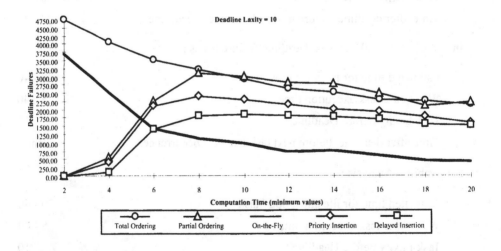

Figure 10. Computation Times

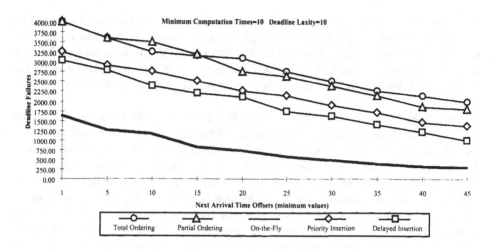

Figure 11. Task Arrival Rates

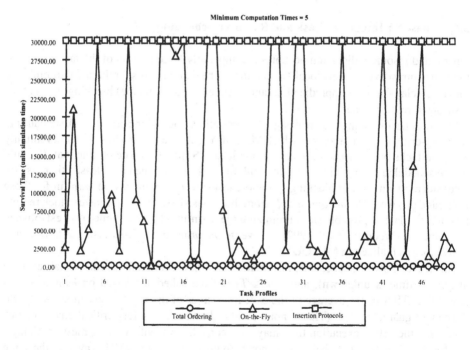

Figure 12. Survivability Analysis

In figure 10, when task computation times are short relative to task next arrival times (next arrival time was kept constant in this figure), then it is *possible* to serve tasks more quickly than they arrive thus avoiding long queues of waiting tasks. Under these conditions, the Priority Insertion, Delayed Insertion and Partial Ordering protocols do well. The Total

Ordering protocol, because of its serial nature, and the On-the-Fly protocol because of its message intensiveness, spend more time engaging in protocol messaging than in executing the tasks when computation times are short relative to communication delays. Though computation times are short, the combined acquisition times and computation times are very long for these protocols, causing them to be unable to schedule tasks as quickly as they arrive.

In all evaluations the new protocols outperformed the *Total Ordering* as well as the similar *Partial Ordering* protocols (Rajkumar, 1989)) very clearly. When survivability of the algorithms was evaluated a significant result was that the Priority Insertion and Delayed Insertion protocols performed superior (surviving throughout the entire simulation run) to the On-the-Fly protocol (fig. 12) which, in turn, was better over a wide range, under the deadline failure rate criterion. We concluded that for distributed safety-critical systems the Delayed Insertion protocol performance was very good, but was excellent in terms of survivability. In our MELODY prototype this protocol is therefore, as part of the FS structure, the resource scheduling feature selected for all subsequent phases. (It was also experimentally verified that all previous findings worked under this FS structure refinement.)

2.4. Phase 5 : Integrated Task and Resource Scheduling

Distributed resource allocation occupies a comparably large portion of the task execution time, in contrast to the purely local TS activities. The major factors for this are the combined message delays and the unpredictable (and remotely uncontrollable) blocking times at the distributed resource sites.

In traditional operating system design resource allocation is done prior to task scheduling. In safety-critical environments in which MELODY is to operate, if a task T_j had eventually acquired locks on all needed file copies, the local TS might then determine that T_j could not be scheduled to finish in time. Although the locks would then be released there is still a considerable amount of blocking of remote tasks by T_j which may be harmful for those tasks, and this would be *uncontrollable* from those task sites. In order to instead lock remote resources as late as possible (for minimizing the harmful effect mentioned) we established the principle (Wedde and Xu, 1992) to **reverse** *the order of task and distributed resource scheduling* as realized in MELODY.

This leaves TS without accurate information on task execution times (the actual resource allocation time is unknown), and a task T_j will be scheduled based on estimates. In MELODY, TS uses the average of the execution times of the last five instances of T_j. So TS cannot guarantee T_j . (This is not a serious drawback in safety-critical environments given that the actual execution time may vary considerably with varying message delays, say for data transfer, such that there is no sharp guarantee anyway.) However, at the same time a task with allocated resources will be mostly guaranteed to complete in time. The job to possibly abort tasks in their resource acquisition phase (whenever it turns out that there would not be enough time left to complete by the deadline) is handled by a new service module, the **Run-Time Monitor (RTM)** module. Every task instance goes through five phases in order to complete its execution (fig. 13). Initially a task instance will be scheduled by TS. *Resource location, allocation and locking* is then performed with the assistance of

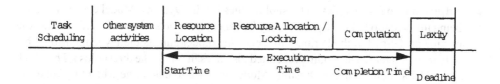

Figure 13. Task Execution Phases

FS, and monitored by RTM. Once a task has locked its resources it would be placed into the execution queue (ordered by TS). After the resource location is over a good estimate for the actual task computation time is known (through the number and location of needed resources), and RTM would use this to monitor the deadline behavior of each task.

Since task scheduling with local resources takes much less time than remote file allocation a trade-off must be made when integrating the TS and FS functions. It is expected that if TS is invoked too frequently the added invocations would result in degraded performance, while delaying invocation for too long would also degrade the performance and, more importantly, the system survivability. As a result, we developed and investigated the following integration models :

- **Periodic Model** : In the first model the TS is invoked periodically after a defined interval of time has passed. (This time interval before the next invocation is conceived to be adaptable for certain time periods, to the changing environmental conditions of task arrival rates. In our experiments we used constant periods only). We denote this model using by Periodic($< period >$).

- **Dynamic Model** : The TS function would not be of much use for scheduling essentially critical task instances since abortion of such tasks potentially causes the whole system to decease. Consequently, in MELODY the new RTM also, while inspecting the TS queue of arrived task instances, picks the essentially critical instances and inserts them (in appropriate scheduling order) into a new FS queue, the *Essentially Critical Request Queue* (**ECR**). (So the essentially critical tasks would bypass TS .) The task instances that are still scheduled by TS - which are critical or non-critical - will be inserted into the *Non-Essential Request Queue* (**NER**) at FS, *after a TS invocation took place*. While ECR and NER together form the set of tasks on which FS operates, ECR has priority over NER . Three dynamic thresholds are used to determine when to invoke the TS:

  - A threshold **FTh** is set for the File Server queue **NER**, as well as two thresholds **STh1** and **STh2** with $Sth1 \leq STh2$ for the TS waiting queue. They monitor the number of newly arrived tasks instances.

  - The Dynamic Model invokes TS whenever both **FTh** has been underpassed and **STh1** has been surpassed, or after **STh2** alone has been surpassed. (The threshold values are again conceived to be adaptable, over certain time intervals, to specifics of the task profiles encountered).

We will denote this model by Dynamic($- \mid FTh, STh1, Sth2$).

- **Adjusted Dynamic Model** : Threshold values for the Dynamic Model can result in TS being invoked too frequently, and it may be beneficial to delay invocation for an interval of time as defined in the Periodic model. This model adjusts the Dynamic Model by only invoking the TS at certain predefined instances in time. The thresholds **FTh, STh1** and **STh2** as defined in the Dynamic Model are used to determine when to invoke the TS, however this model delays invocation until the next period (defined in the Periodic model). It is denoted as Adjusted Dynamic($< period >| FTh, STh1, STh2$).

- **Joined Model** : Using the features of both Periodic Model and Dynamic Model the TS will be invoked after either a periodic time interval, or may be invoked earlier using the thresholds of the Dynamic model. This model is denoted Joined($< period >| FTh, STh1, STh2$).

The main expectation for the new integrated task and resource scheduling policies is that the lack of guarantee by TS would be more than made up by the less chaotic and harmful way of early resource locking, as used in traditional operating system design. Our first concern was to compare any of the new integrated models with a **Classical Model** of periodic TS invocation and resource scheduling prior to task scheduling. This was subject to extensive simulation experiments reported in (Wedde et al., 1994).

We expected that the Periodic Model would have an optimal setting of the invocation period with respect to the deadline failure rate, and this performance would degrade as the period was increased or decreased from the optimum. For the Dynamic Model there should also be optimal settings for FTh, STh1 and Sth2. Also, the combined integration methods (Joined Model and Adjusted Dynamic Model) had been developed to assure that under certain extreme settings their performance would be matching the one of one of its constituent models. For example, a very long period for the Joined Model would cause it to no longer be influenced by the period, and as a result perform nearly identical to the Dynamic Model. In contrast, the Adjusted Dynamic Model, under a very short period, would probably match the performance of the Dynamic Model. Using these expectations, other features of the Joined Model and Adjusted Dynamic Model could then securely be evaluated, and separated from the effects discussed.

Experimental Set-Up : The task profiles used here are the same as described in section 2.2. In the subsequent discussion (fig. 14 through 25) we restrict ourselves to task profiles in which all tasks are initially critical, with values ranging from 5-8, and sensitivity values were picked randomly between 2 and 8. We varied the characteristic parameters $< period >$, FTh, $STh1$, and $STh2$ in the following ways: the $< period >$ values were set to 55, 70, 85, 100, and 115 units of time. The threshold FTh was chosen to be either 1, 5, 10, 15, 20, 25. $STh1$ was set to 1, 5, 10, 15, 20, or 25, and $STh2$ was set to be 1, 5, 20, 35, 50, or 65. *We also varied all specific integration parameters widely beyond the displayed limits. This did not change any tendency as observed in the experiments with the parameter ranges selected above. Thus the settings chosen for the discussion here can be considered as representative for a much wider range.*

In all experiments the **Classical Model** performed very poorly. Even in the best case 90% of tasks failed to meet their deadlines. For periods over 70 it reached 100% failures through the experimental duration (30,000 units of time). The picture becomes even worse by recognizing that in fig. 14 the classical model has 95% of overall deadline misses. As for *survivability*, already during the first simulation interval an essentially critical task cannot be completed in time so that the systems do not survive. (This was the same in all other eperiments discussed but was not displayed for better scaling of the other comparative results.) Since the criticality of the tasks is leaning towards non-criticalness as described in the previous paragraph, there is a drastic difference with respect to all our own integration models: These survive under all circumstances (even with up to 50% total deadline misses) while the Classical Model *is completely useless even under moderate survivability constraints. It was quite evident that MELODY's reversed order of task and resource scheduling is not only advantageous but necessary in an unpredictable environment.*

The **Periodic Model**'s performance is optimal for a period of 70 (fig. 15). However, its performance degrades significantly as the period is increased or decreased (figures 14 and 16). This optimal interval of 70 was directly related to the task profile selected as we found by studying various different profiles.

In the **Dynamic Model** the period is not utilized and its performance is unchanged in figures 14-16. In Figures 17-19, threshold FTh is varied from 5 to 15, showing an optimal setting of FTh to be 10 (fig. 18). However, as FTh is increased or decreased the models performance degrades significantly, resulting from the infrequent invocation of TS (fig. 17). Figures 20-22 show an optimal setting for STh1 (fig. 21). The Dynamic Model's performance degradation can be seen as STh1 is increased or decreased (figures 20 and 22). Setting STh2 to 5 (fig. 23) enhances the performance of the Dynamic Model due to poor performance of the settings for FTh and STh1, however significant degradation is shown as STh2 is increased (fig. 24-25).

Figure 16 shows that long periods for the **Adjusted Dynamic Model** causes the performance of this model to degrade in comparison to the Dynamic Model, while short periods causes it match the Dynamic Model's performance (fig. 14). Increasing FTh causes the Dynamic Model to increase its invocation to a point where the task scheduler is invoked too frequently (fig. 19), causing the Adjusted Dynamic Model to perform identical to the Periodic Model. In figures 20-22, *the Adjusted Dynamic Model's performance worsens due to the longer delay occurred as a result of increasing STh1*(fig. 22). STh2 has significant impact on the performance of the Dynamic Model, while it had less of an impact on this model's performance since the period eventually keeps this model from improving its performance to the same degree as the Dynamic Model (fig. 24).

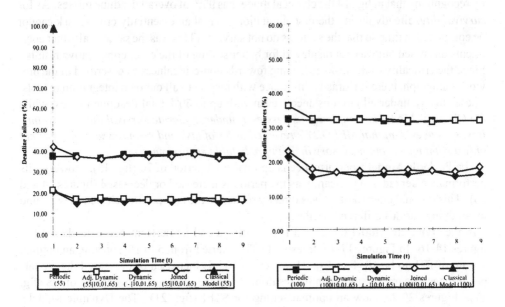

Figure 14. TS Integration Period=55

Figure 16. TS Integration Period=100

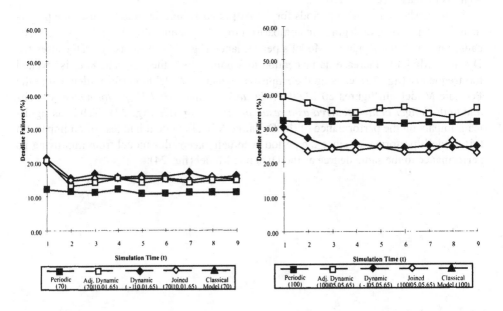

Figure 15. TS Integration Period=70

Figure 17. TS Integration Fth=05

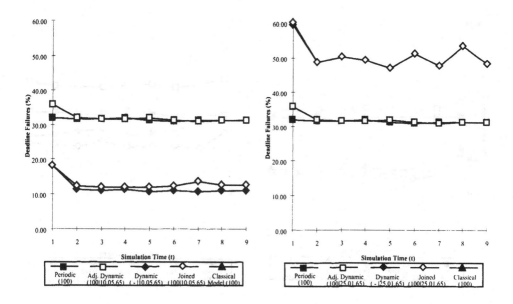

Figure 18. TS Integration Fth=10

Figure 20. TS Integration STh1=01

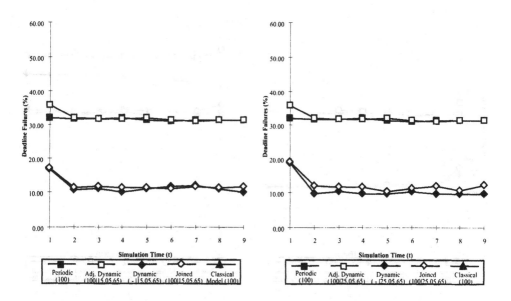

Figure 19. TS Integration Fth=15

Figure 21. TS Integration Sth1=05

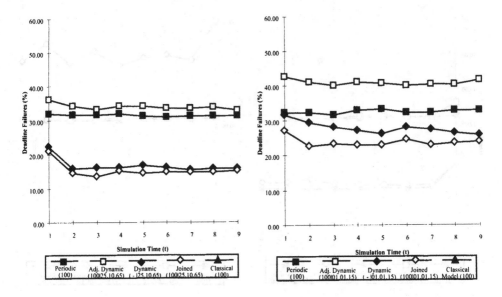

Figure 22. TS Integration Sth1=10

Figure 24. TS Integration Sth2=15

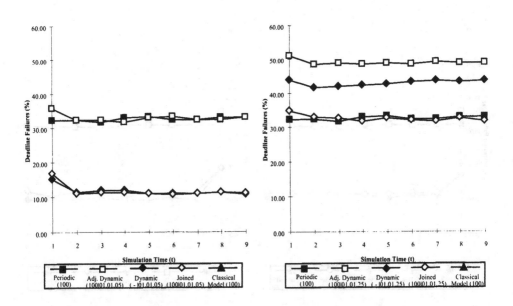

Figure 23. TS Integration Sth2=05

Figure 25. TS Integration Sth2=25

Short periods for the **Joined Model** had a significant impact on the performance causing it to match the poor performance of the Periodic Model (fig. 14), while long periods caused the performance to eventually match that of the Dynamic Model (fig. 16). In figure 19, the Dynamic Model invokes the task scheduler too often, and the Joined Model's performance is slightly worse due to the added invocations caused by the period of 70 (fig. 19).

Overall the Periodic Model never outperformed all of the other models. The Dynamic Model was never the worst of all models, and only under certain extreme setting is its performance poor. Throughout nearly all of the charts its performance is the better or nearly the same as one of the other models. The Adjusted Dynamic Model was able to improve the performance of the Dynamic Model significantly under certain parameter ranges, however in cases with long periods its performance was consistently worse than the one of the Dynamic Model. The Joined Model's performance for short periods was directly related to the increased invocations resulting from a short period, while longer periods caused there to be performance improvement from the Dynamic Model. Under conditions were the Periodic Model and Dynamic Model were not invoking TS often enough there was an improvement under the Joined Model. In our current prototype implementation we use the Dynamic Model.

3. Conclusions and Future Work

In this paper we have given an outline of our method called *Incremental Experimentation*, and how it was used in the development of our MELODY distributed operating system. Incremental Experimentation was designed as a heuristic methodology for systematically designing and analyzing complex safety-critical systems in the unavoidable absence of a closed-form approach. This development has proceeded from the initial design of the MELODY file system, through the refinements of criticality and sensitivity, the creation of unique distributed resource scheduling algorithms, and most recently the integration of task and resource scheduling. Every single model feature was developed under well justified expectations derived from experiments in a well understood and well investigated previous model context. In the extended model the previous behavior and performance picture could be obtained through particular parameter settings or ranges, either in the model settings or with respect to task/data profiles. For the refined model the novel behavioral properties could then unambiguously be attributed to, and characterized as, the influences of the novel system parameters. (This was particularly clear when the reversed order of task and resource scheduling was introduced and discussed.)

Besides making the integration policies sensitive with respect to task criticality and sensitivity as already mentioned, the next step of the current MELODY system project is under operation in our labs. It constitutes a major model extension, from simulation to **distributed experiments** that explicitly reflect actual communication delays. To this end, *communication deadlines* have been introduced into MELODY, for coping with the unpredictability and heterogeneity of message traffic and delays under hard real-time constraints. This is realized on a Token Ring network of 9 IBM RS/6000 workstations, in our Distributed Operating Systems Lab at the University of Dortmund, and is subject to forthcoming publications.

Acknowledgments

The comments of the unknown referees are highly appreciated.

References

D.C. Daniels, "The Design and Analysis of Protocols for Distributed Resource Scheduling under Real-Time Constraints"; Ph.D. Dissertation; Wayne State University, June 1992

J.W. Havender, "Avoiding Deadlocks in Multitasking Systems"; *IBM Systems Journal*, Vol. 7, No. 2, (1968)

D. Haban, K. Shin, "Application of Real-Time Monitoring to Scheduling Tasks with Random Execution Times"; *IEEE Trans. on Software Engineering*; Vol. 16 No. 12; 1990

F. Jahanian, R. Rajkumar, S. Raju, "Runtime Monitoring of Timing Constraints in Distributed Real-Time Systems"; *Real-Time Systems*; Vol. 7. No. 3 (1994)

R. Rajkumar, "Task Synchronization in Real-Time Systems"; Ph.D. Dissertation, Department of Electrical and Computer Engineering, Canegie Mellon University, 1989

H.F. Wedde, G.S. Alijani, D. Huizinga, G. Kang, B. K. Kim, "MELODY: A Completely Decentralized Adaptive File System for Handling Real-Time Tasks in Unpredictable Environments"; *Real-Time Systems*; Vol. 2 No. 4(1990)

H.F. Wedde, D.C. Daniels, D. Huizinga, "Efficient Distributed Resource Scheduling for Adaptive Real-Time Operating System Support"; *Springer Lecture Notes in Computer Science*; Vol. 497 (1991)

H.F. Wedde, B. Korel, J.A. Lind, "Highly Integrated Task and Resource Scheduling for Mission-Critical Systems"; Proc. of the EUROMICRO'93 Workshop on Real-Time Systems; Oulu, Finland, June 1993

H.F. Wedde, "Real-Time Operating Systems and Software: State-of-the-Art and Future Challenges"; *Encyclopedia of Microcomputers*, Vol. 14 (S. 255), Marcel Dekker Inc., New York, NY 1994

H.F. Wedde, J.A. Lind, A. Eiss, "Achieving Dependability in Safety-critical Operating Systems Through Adaptability and Large-Scale Functional Integration"; Proc. of the ICPADS'94 International Conference on Parallel and Distributed Systems; Hsinchu, Taiwan, December, 1994

H.F. Wedde, M. Xu, "Scheduling Critical and Sensitive Tasks with Remote Requests in Safety-Critical Systems"; Proc. of the EUROMICRO'92 Workshop on Real-Time Systems; Athens, Greece, June 1992

J. Xu, D.L.Parnas, "On Satisfying Timing Constraints in Hard Real-Time Systems"; *IEEE-TSE* Vol.19 No.1 (1993)

Real-Time Systems, 13, 303–306 (1997)

Contributing Authors

Bernd Krämer was born in Berlin, Germany, in 1947. He is a full professor at FernUniversität in Hagen, where he holds the chair of data processing. He is also a director of INTE, a consulting division of the university's Electrical Engineering faculty. He obtained his doctorate in computer science from the Technical University of Berlin where he also studied electrical engineering and computer science from 1969 to 1975. From 1975 to 1989 he was a senior researcher and project leader at the German National Research Institute of Computer Science. From 1989 to 1990 he was an adjunct research professor at Naval Postgraduate School in Monterey, California.

He has research experiences in formal software specification, design, and analysis, in software process technology, and in real-time systems. His current research interests include development methods and tools for high integrity software, networked heterogeneous multimedia, and distributed software engineering and management. He is on the editorial board of the Journal on High Integrity Systems, the Journal on Software Engineering and Knowledge Engineering, and the Journal of Integrated Design and Process Technology.

Hans Langmaack born in 1934, studied mathematics, physics and logics 1954–60 at U Münster and U Freiburg. In 1960 he received his Dr. rer. nat. at U Münster and in 1967 his Habilitation at TU Munich, both degrees in mathematics.

From 1960–66 he worked as a scientific assistant to Prof. K. Samelson and Prof. F.L. Bauer at the mathematical institutes of U Mainz and TU Munich. From 1966–67 he was an assistant professor at the computer science department of Purdue U, Lafayette, Ind., USA. From 1967–70 he taught as a Dozent at TU Munich. From 1970–74 he held a chair for informatics at U Saarbr"ucken. Since 1974 he is an ord. professor for informatics at U Kiel.

H. Langmaack's research areas are programming language semantics, compiler construction, program correctness proof calculi and their completeness, provably correct computer based systems.

Jon A. Lind received a B.S. degree from the University of Oregon, in 1989, and an M.Sc. degree from Wayne State University, in 1993. From 1989 to 1993, he worked for Electronic Data System at the General Motors Headquarters in Detroit, Michigan. He is currently pursuing the Ph.D. in Computer Science at the University of Dortmund, Germany, where he is a Research Assistant with the Institute of Operating Systems and Computer Architecture.

J. Lind's current research interests include mission-critical systems and distributed operating systems.

Antonio Mazzeo was born in Italy in 1949. In 1976 he received the Dr. Ing. Degree in electronic engineering from the University of Palermo, Italy. Since 1976 he has been with the Department of Computer Science of the University of Naples where he became Full Professor in 1994. He is a consultant for companies in Italy and Europe. His research interests are in the areas of parallel and distributed architectures, distributed languages, operating systems, programming environments and performance evaluation.

Nicola Mazzocca graduated in electronic engineering at the University of Naples in 1987. He spent one year at Ansaldo Trasporti where he worked on the design of process control systems. In 1988 he joined the Department of Computer Science of the University of Naples, where he received his Ph.D. in Computer Science. He currently is assistant professor at the Department of Computer Science of the University of Naples. His research interests include performance evaluation of parallel architectures, special purpose architectures for signal processing, and implementation of programming languages for parallel and distributed systems.

Stefano Russo is assistant professor at the Department of Computer Science and Systems of University of Naples, Italy, where he received the Degree cum laude in Electronic Engineering and the Ph.D. in Computer Science in 1988 and 1993, respectively. His research interests are in the areas of software engineering for parallel and distributed systems, and of high performance network computing.

Valeria Vittorini was born in Naples, Italy in 1965. She received her Doctor degree in Mathematics from the University of Naples in 1990 and her Ph.D. degree in Computer Science from the same University in 1996. Currently she is assistant professor at the Computer Science Department of the second University of Naples. Her research interests include real-time and dependability systems, distributed applications, formal methods in system specification and design.

Norbert Völker graduated in Mathematics at the University of Bochum in 1988. After being a research member of the Dutch STOP project (Specification and Transformation of Programs), he is now affiliated with the Electrotechnical Department of the FernUniversität Hagen, Germany. He is currently working on his PhD in Computer Science in the area of theorem prover based verification of reactive systems.

Horst F. Wedde received the B.Sc. and M.S. (Diploma) degree in Pure Mathematics, the Ph.D. degree in Computer Science (1974), all from the University of Bonn, Germany. His appointments included a Senior Research Staff position at the Gesellschaft für Mathematik und Datenverarbeitung (GMD) in Bonn, Germany (1969–83), visiting professor positions at the universities of Pisa (1980) and Turin (1982), Italy, and at the Academy of Sciences in Warsaw, Poland (1977, 1980). Prof. Wedde was on faculty of Wayne

State University/Detroit (1984–1993). From this time on, he is with the School of Computer Science of the University of Dortmund, Germany, where he holds the Chair of Operating Systems

Dr. Wedde's major research interests, as well as numerous publications, are in various areas of Distributed Computing Systems including Theory, Distributed Operating/File Systems, Distributed Real-Time Systems.

Prof. Wedde served as the General Chair for the IEEE-RTOSS'93 Workshop, as a Program Vice Chair for the IEEE-ICDCS'89 and COMPSAC'92 conferences, and on numerous program committees of relevant US and European conferences in his fields of interest. He is the Program Chair of the 1997 EUROMICRO Workshop on Real-Time Systems in Toledo (Spain). He was on the Advisory Editorial Board of *Computing* from 1991 through 1994.

Dr. Wedde is a member of ACM, IEEE Computer Society, and GI. He was the Editor of the *Real-Time Systems Newsletter* of the IEEE Technical Committee on Real-Time Systems from 1987 until 1994.